# CLAIM YOUR FREE "FROM EXPERTISE TO IMPACT" SUCCESS BUNDLE

I've created a special bonus resources package to support you in applying the "policy mindset" taught in this book to use your scientific and technical knowledge to enhance society and to determine your place in science and technology policy.

- ☑ Fillable PDF Workbook Version of From Expertise to Impact

## AND FREE E-BOOKS LIKE

- ☑ Does Your Science and Technology Policy Guidance Get Ignored?
- ☑ Identify a Science & Technology Policy Career You Love in 4 Simple and Practical Steps
- ☑ Have the Societal Impact You Want as an Executive S&T Policymaker With Your Scientific and Technical Expertise
- ☑ Establish Your Science and Technology Policy Consulting Business

## AND VIDEOS LIKE

- ☑ What is Science and Technology Policy?
- ☑ Assessing the Impact: Evaluation of Public Programs
- ☑ Leveraging AI to Enhance the Quality and Efficiency of Your Science & Technology Policy Activities: An Exploration of ChatGPT Applications
- ☑ What is Equity Analysis and How Can I Use It to Help Reach Societal Goals?

This resource bundle is my no-cost-whatsoever gift to you.

**GO TO SCITECHPOLICYACADEMY.COM/RESOURCES TO CLAIM IT!**

# FROM EXPERTISE TO IMPACT

Copyright © 2024 by
Deborah D. Stine, PhD

Paperback ISBN: 978-1-63337-797-4
E-Book ISBN: 978-1-63337-908-4

All rights reserved.
This book, or parts thereof, may not be reproduced in any form without permission.

# FROM EXPERTISE TO IMPACT

## A PRACTICAL GUIDE TO INFORMING AND INFLUENCING SCIENCE AND TECHNOLOGY POLICY

### DEBORAH D. STINE, PhD

Founder, Science and Technology Policy Academy

# Table of Contents

**Introduction** ............................................................................................................. 1
    Mind the Gap: Recognizing the Science-Policy Divide ............................................. 1
    Missed Opportunities, Gained Policy Insights ............................................................ 2
    Turning Research into Results: A Path to Societal Impact for Scientists
    and Engineers ................................................................................................................. 3

**Chapter 1: What Is Science and Technology Policy?** ................................................ 4
    How Is Science and Technology (S&T) Policy Defined? ............................................. 5
    Are You Interested in "Policy for S&T" or "S&T for Policy"? ....................................... 7
    What Is Policy Analysis? ................................................................................................ 9
    What Happens If Policies Are Implemented without Analysis? ............................... 10
    What Are the Steps in Policy Analysis? ...................................................................... 10
    The 4Es: Effectiveness, Efficiency, Equity, Ease of Political Acceptability ............... 11
    Developing Your Own Policy Analysis ........................................................................ 14
    Thought Exercise 1: How Do You Make Decisions? .................................................. 15

**Chapter 2: Step 1: Describe the Societal Problem** ................................................. 16
    Identifying a Manageable Societal Problem for Your Policy Analysis .................... 17
        What Societal Problem Are You Trying to Solve? ................................................ 17
        What Are the Root Causes of the Societal Problem,
        According to Stakeholders? ................................................................................... 18
        What Are Possible Solutions to the Societal Problem,
        According to Stakeholders? ................................................................................... 18
        Where Might Analysis Play a Role in Developing the
        Optimal Policy to Mitigate Those Root Causes? .................................................. 19
        What Is the Geographic Focus of Your Analysis? ................................................ 19
        What Policymakers Are the Best Focus for Your Analysis? ................................ 19
        Are There Any Upcoming Relevant Policy Activities? ......................................... 21
    Food Insecurity Example ............................................................................................. 21
    Tip: Narrow Your Policy Focus .................................................................................... 23
    Thought Exercise 2: Societal Challenge of Interest to You ...................................... 24

## Chapter 3: Step 2: Develop Your "What Actions, If Any" Policy Question ............27
### Challenges in Developing Your S&T Policy Analysis ..............................................27
### Policy Question Model: "What Actions, If Any" ....................................................28
#### Good Question ..........................................................................................30
#### Bad Question ...........................................................................................30
### Food Insecurity Example ...........................................................................32
### Tip: Get Feedback on Your Question ........................................................32
### Thought Exercise 3: Develop Your "What Actions, If Any" Policy Question ............33

## Chapter 4: Step 3: Identify Two Policy Options in Addition to the Status Quo ......34
### Gather Stakeholder Opinions on the Status Quo ......................................35
### Identify Parallel Policies in Other Regions ................................................37
### Develop and Seek "Out-of-the-Box" Policies ............................................39
### Picking Your Two Options for Analysis ......................................................41
### Food Insecurity Example ...........................................................................42
### Tip: Go Beyond Your Own Policy Ideas ....................................................43
### Thought Exercise 4: Identify Two Policy Options to Analyze ....................44

## Chapter 5: Step 4: Analyze the Effectiveness of the Status Quo and the Policy Options ..............................................................................................45
### Develop a Logic Model for the Status Quo ...............................................46
### Modify the Status Quo Logic Model with Policy Option Activities ............49
### Develop a Pro/Con Effectiveness Analysis of Status Quo and Policy Options ......50
### Food Insecurity Example ...........................................................................52
### Tip: Look for Effectiveness Analysis in Gray Literature ............................53
### Thought Exercise 5: Develop Your Pro/Con Analysis of the Effectiveness of the Status Quo and Two Policy Options ................................................................55

## Chapter 6: Step 5: Analyze the Efficiency of the Status Quo and the Policy Options ..............................................................................................56
### What Is Benefit-Cost Analysis? ..................................................................58
### Find Benefit-Cost Analysis ........................................................................59
### Develop a Pro/Con Efficiency Analysis of Status Quo and Policy Options ...........59
### Food Insecurity Example ...........................................................................60
### Tip: Ballpark Benefit-Cost Analysis Is Better than No Analysis .................64
### Thought Exercise 6: Develop Your Pro/Con Analysis of the Efficiency of the Status Quo and Two Policy Options ................................................................65

## Chapter 7: Step 6: Analyze the Equity of the Status Quo and the Policy Options ... 66
- What Is Equity? ... 69
- Develop an Equity Analysis ... 70
- Develop a Pro/Con Equity Analysis of Status Quo and Policy Options ... 72
- Food Insecurity Example ... 73
- Tip: Equity Is More Than Demographics ... 75
- Thought Exercise 7: Develop Your Pro/Con Analysis of the Equity of the Status Quo and Two Policy Options ... 76

## Chapter 8: Step 7: Analyze the Ease of Political Acceptability of the Status Quo and the Policy Options ... 77
- What Is Meant by Ease of Political Acceptability? ... 78
- Assess the Ease of Political Acceptability of the Policy Options ... 79
- Develop a Pro/Con Ease of Acceptability Analysis of the Status Quo and Two Options ... 84
- Food Insecurity Example ... 84
- Tip: Not Everyone Will Love Your Policy Options ... 87
- Thought Exercise 8: Develop Your Pro/Con Analysis of the Ease of Political Acceptability of the Status Quo and Two Policy Options ... 89

## Chapter 9: Step 8: Synthesize the Results of the 4E Analysis ... 90
- Develop a Pro/Con Table Bringing Together Your 4E Analysis ... 91
- Food Insecurity Example ... 92
- Tip: Yes, You Can Adjust Your Analysis ... 92
- Thought Exercise 9: Bring Your 4E Analysis Together ... 94

## Chapter 10: Step 9: Decide What Policy Option(s) to Present or Recommend ... 95
- Decide! ... 97
- Food Insecurity Example ... 98
- Tip: The Status Quo May Be the Best Option ... 100
- Thought Exercise 10: Make Your Recommendation ... 101

## Chapter 11: Step 10: Communicate the Results of Your Analysis ... 102
- How Should You Communicate Your Analysis? ... 103
- Developing Your Message ... 103
- Decide which communication methods to use for each audience ... 103
- Focus on your message, not on policy background or analytical methods ... 106
- Put Your Bottom Line Up Front (BLUF) ... 106

Don't use jargon .................................................................................................................108
Employ the 3Cs in Writing: Clear, Concise, Coherent ..............................................110
    Clear ...........................................................................................................................110
    Concise .......................................................................................................................111
    Coherent ....................................................................................................................111
Employ the 3Rs in Speaking: Relevance, Real-World Impact, Results .....................112
Disseminating Your Message ...................................................................................112
    1. Make a list of people who constitute the audience for your message .......114
    2. Develop a variety of dissemination products and events ...........................114
    3. Timing is important .........................................................................................114
Food Insecurity Example ..........................................................................................115
Tip: Making Public Policy Is Difficult and Time-Consuming ...................................118
Thought Exercise 11: Develop Your One-Minute Policy Pitch .................................120

## Chapter 12: What's Next for Your Science and Technology Policy Journey? .........121
Ways to Inform and Influence Policymakers ...........................................................121
What Are Common Obstacles to Having a Societal Impact
and How Can You Overcome Them? .......................................................................122
    Unclear "ask" .............................................................................................................122
    Not researching your audience and their position on your issue ....................123
    Making assumptions about or looking down on policymakers
    and their staff ...........................................................................................................124
Gaining a Policy Mindset .........................................................................................125

## Appendix A: Brief History of Science and Technology Policy in the United States .................................................................................................128

## Appendix B: How Do You Want to Engage with Policymakers? ..............................131

## Appendix C: Challenges You May Face in Bringing Your Expertise to Policymaking .........................................................................................................134

## Appendix D: Resources ..............................................................................................137

## Appendix E: West Virginia Carbon Dioxide Reduction Example .............................139

About the Author .......................................................................................................140
About the Science and Technology Policy Academy .............................................142
Endnotes ....................................................................................................................143

## Introduction

As a high school student, I was passionate about the environment, and I was lucky enough to apply that passion in San Antonio, Texas, through a National Science Foundation (NSF) summer program that allowed me to conduct research for the first time in a real lab. My focus was on microbial degradation of oil, a natural way to clean up oil from saltwater environments.

I cared about this issue because every summer when I went to Padre Island, a barrier island in the Gulf of Mexico, I would get spots of oil on my swimsuit whenever I went into the water. If this happened to me, I could just imagine how that oil affected the wildlife that lived in the Gulf every day of their life. This background oil in the Gulf's waters would likely increase over time, and any oil spills that occurred would just make the situation worse. So what was needed was a continual system for removing oil from the Gulf, not just a one-time fix. I hoped my research on the topic could clean up this oil on a long-term basis. This would improve a number of societal outcomes, including protecting humans and the Gulf's ecology, but also contribute to the economic development of the region—who wants to go to a beach in these conditions?

I quickly learned, however, that conducting research and writing a scientific paper based on that research was not enough. My high school mind had not thought beyond getting the research done and producing a scientific paper. I didn't think about the next steps beyond that. So when I did go back to Padre Island, the oil (unsurprisingly) was still there.

## Mind the Gap: Recognizing the Science-Policy Divide

I blamed the policymakers for not taking care of the problem, questioning why they didn't use methods like microbial degradation to clean up the oil. That was faulty reasoning. However, the challenge was with me and other scientists and engineers not going beyond what we were required to do to get published. How could I expect policymakers to take action when the community didn't do the analysis needed for them to do so?

## Introduction

Thus began my lifelong journey to understand how to use my scientific and technical expertise to have an impact on society. To do that, I would need to think like a policymaker and provide the analysis and products they needed to take action.

### Missed Opportunities, Gained Policy Insights

Here's what I did wrong back then, and perhaps you are doing wrong today if you want your scientific and technical expertise to have an impact on society.

First, my paper covered only the scientific and technical aspects of the situation. I didn't take the next steps to think about how that research might be put into action and include that in my paper.

Second, I didn't produce easy-to-understand documents that policymakers and the public could use to encourage the implementation of this method to clean up oil.

Third, I didn't share any of my findings with those in a position to take action. I should have reached out to policymakers and public organizations that cared about oil pollution in the Gulf of Mexico. How could I expect anyone other than the scientific and technical community to know about my work if I didn't share it with them?

Out of curiosity, I typed in the focus of my high school research, "microbial degradation of oil," into Google today to see if anything has happened in the field since then. Interestingly, many researchers are still focused on the topic and producing research results not that dissimilar to what I did decades ago. These researchers, however, are frequently making the same mistakes I did, as outlined above.

I did find a ray of hope in my search, however, that research over decades can contribute to responding to societal challenges. You might remember the 2010 Deepwater Horizon (DWH) oil spill that, like my research, focused on the Gulf of Mexico. I was working for the White House at that point during the Obama administration, and others in my office and at the broader federal, state, and local levels were contributing their scientific and technical knowledge to cleaning up the spill. So did that knowledge make a difference?

Yes, it did! A 2020 analysis entitled "How Microbes Clean up Oil: Lessons From the Deepwater Horizon Oil Spill," written by experts from several scientific and technical societies, found that "the wealth and diversity of microbes in the oceans undoubtedly contributed to ecosystem recovery after DWH, and our ability to capture and study those processes will help provide data-driven solutions to future environmental challenges."[1]

## Turning Research into Results: A Path to Societal Impact for Scientists and Engineers

In this book, we will discover that informing and influencing policymakers is not just confined to the scientific elite. It is, in fact, a skill that can be learned just like the science and engineering knowledge and skills you learned in college. Few science and engineering professors, however, teach you how to take the next steps so you can have an impact on society with your scientific and technical expertise.

This book will help you do just that. I encourage you not just to read this book, but to "earn by doing" through the thought exercises at the end of each chapter. Just as you needed to practice what you learned in your science, engineering, and mathematics classes by doing homework and lab activities, the same is true for learning how to inform and influence policymakers with your scientific and technical expertise.

After reading this book, not only will you discover your ability to use your scientific and technical skills to better understand the policymaking process, but you will understand the role you want to play in science and technology policymaking. You will also gain an understanding of who you are, as a representative of the science and technology community, as a person, and as a leader others will follow into the world of science and technology policy. You will have the policy mindset that will move you from someone with expertise to someone with impact.

# Chapter 1: What Is Science and Technology Policy?

My first foray into the world of science and technology policy began without me even being aware of what it was about. All I knew was that I wanted to improve environmental quality. This societal goal led to me earning a degree in mechanical and environmental engineering at the University of California, Irvine, in southern California. This was a great place to focus on air pollution issues, renewable energy, and ways to reduce pollution because of its long-term air pollution problems and the many actions taken to mitigate it. Although I did not take any classes in political science, I did learn about environmental policy as part of my engineering education.

A major change in environmental policy took place during those years when Ronald Reagan became president of the United States, replacing Jimmy Carter. Their views on the environment could not have been more different. When Jimmy Carter, trained as an engineer, became president, he strongly advocated for renewable energy sources, provided incentives for their use, encouraged Americans to become more energy efficient, and signed into law the establishment of the U.S. Department of Energy.

By the time I graduated from college, Ronald Reagan was president. His view of science and technology policy was far different from that of President Carter. The saying that "80 percent of air pollution comes from plants and trees" is attributed to Reagan. He also cut the budget and staff of the U.S. Environmental Protection Agency, saying that air pollution laws were detrimental to the industrial growth of the coal and steel industries and that this instead came from nature, including the previously mentioned trees as well as the 1980 Mount Saint Helens eruption.

These actions spurred my interest in making an impact on policy with my engineering expertise and in learning more about how public policy is made. (Perhaps a similar situation about a policy you cared about also led to your interest in S&T policy.)

After college, I got my first real engineering job as a field engineer for Texas's air pollution agency at a regional office in Beaumont, Texas. At that time, the Beaumont region (which includes Port Neches and Port Arthur, east of Houston) had some of the largest oil refineries and chemical plants in the country, most of them built in World War II.

## What Is Science and Technology Policy?

Overall, the locals felt pretty positively toward these plants, and frequent odors were nicknamed "the smell of money."

During my time there, I began understanding the importance of S&T policy (still without knowing what it really was) to members of the public. As a field engineer, I knew that part of my job was to respond to citizen complaints, even in the middle of the night. A frequent complaint was when big tankers would come to gather the naphtha (a chemical) kept in storage tanks with floating roofs. As the product left the tanks, the roof would lower, exposing nearby residents to the strong, mothball-like smell of naphtha. Some of these individuals lived right on the fenceline of the refineries. If I smelled it myself, I could give a notice of violation to the chemical company. But issuing a notice was a challenge because by the time I got there, the odor was often gone.

Years later, at the National Academies of Sciences, Engineering, and Medicine, I ended up working on a study called *Science and Judgment in Risk Assessment*,[2] requested by Congress to review how the EPA conducted risk assessments of hazardous air pollutants. One key assumption in risk analysis, defined in public policy, was the maximum time an individual was exposed to a chemical. The policy question was what risk analysts should assume for the "maximum time." While some questioned if someone would really live on the fenceline of a chemical plant, 24 hours a day, for their entire life, I had actually met these individuals in Beaumont. These families inherited the house in which they were born, lived on the fenceline, and were exposed to chemicals on a regular basis throughout their lives. Later the area where these people lived would be called the "cancer belt." I was able to convey that experience to the expert committee working on this report—bringing some "real-world" information to those who had probably never set foot in Beaumont or perhaps any refinery or chemical plant.

Ever since that time, I've viewed myself as a translator—identifying on behalf of policymakers and the public what "real-world" scientific and technical questions and experiences they have, and conveying scientific and technical knowledge to policymakers and the public so they can make informed decisions.

### How Is Science and Technology (S&T) Policy Defined?

Interestingly, there is no formal definition of science and technology policy despite its long history. (If you'd like to know more about S&T policy history, see Appendix A.)

Here's my definition based on that of an international group of scholars convened by the Organization for Economic Cooperation and Development (OECD) in 1971.[3] As you read through this definition and the table that follows, think about what S&T policy topics are of most interest to you and in what category they fall. Science and technology (S&T) policy includes:

(1) "Policy for S&T," how policymakers manage and fund science, technology, engineering, and mathematics (STEM) research, education, and workforce development; and

(2) "S&T for policy," providing STEM knowledge and expertise to help policymakers develop evidence-based policies that enhance society and solve societal problems.

In simple terms, it's about how governments support science and technology, and how they use science and technology to make better policies. This table provides an overview of each, with examples.

### The Relationship among Science, Technology, and Policymaking

|  | Public Policy Influencing Science and Technology ("Policy for S&T") | Science and Technology Informing Public Policy ("S&T for Policy") |
|---|---|---|
| **Science** | **Policy for Science:** a policymaker's decision as to whether to fund or manage scientific research | **Science for Policy:** a policymaker's decision on how to use scientific analysis in policymaking |
| **Illustrative Examples** | How much public funding should support climate change research, and how should policymakers prioritize that research funding? | Use of scientific information to understand the impacts of climate change and develop policies to adapt to that change |
| **Technology** | **Policy for Technology:** a policymaker's decision as to whether to fund or manage technical research | **Technology for Policy:** a policymaker's decision as to the degree to which to use technical analysis in policymaking |
| **Illustrative Examples** | How much public versus private funding should support research into self-driving cars? | How should self-driving cars be regulated to protect public safety? |

## What Is Science and Technology Policy?

As you forge your own journey in science and technology policy, you're going to find this distinction useful in defining what role you wish to play in public policy on a given societal challenge.

Understanding the difference between the two is also important in calibrating your interactions with policymakers. For example, if you are meeting with a policymaker to describe or advocate for more research funding for your field, you are no different than any other constituent advocating for more funding for the issues they care about, such as reducing hunger, increasing employment, and helping veterans with disabilities.

On the other hand, if the purpose of your meeting is to provide scientific and technical information and guidance that can reduce hunger, increase employment, and help veterans with disabilities, your reception from policymakers is likely to be more positive because you are providing information the policymaker can use to make better decisions.

For now, I'd just like you to think about what aspect of science and technology policy is of most interest to you now. Is it "policy for S&T" or "S&T for policy"?

### Are You Interested in "Policy for S&T" or "S&T for Policy"?

I've worked in both. Although my initial contract to work as a program officer was only for 18 months, I ended up staying at the National Academies of Science, Engineering, and Medicine for 18 years. The first and last studies that I staffed at NASEM, both requested by Congress, provide good illustrations of the difference between the two aspects and will hopefully help you decide on the one in which you're most interested today. This will help you pick the societal topic you'll focus on for the thought analysis you'll do as you go through each step of the policy analysis process.

The first study, entitled *Policy Implications of Greenhouse Warming: Mitigation, Adaptation, and the Science Base*,[4] falls into the category of S&T for policy. The report began by providing a clear understanding of what science tells us about the impact of climate change, as well as the things science was still uncertain about at the time. This data was communicated in such a way that policymakers could make informed decisions about the necessity of taking action.

The study then provided a realistic assessment, with cost estimates, of the possible actions that could be taken by policymakers to reduce greenhouse emissions for everything from agriculture to energy to population control as well as actions to reduce carbon dioxide in the atmosphere. Importantly, the study prioritized the actions that would have the most impact in mitigating climate change based on their cost-effectiveness.

Finally, it described what the possible impact of climate change would be on humans and ecosystems and what actions policymakers would need to take so communities were ready for climate change should it occur.

That study did have an impact in advancing thinking on the issue—particularly in developing the concept of a cost-effectiveness curve[5] and introducing the geoengineering option—but did not result in policy action at the time. Of course, the challenges of climate change are still an issue today. These concepts, however, are still actively contributing to today's public policy dialogues at an international level.

The last study I directed, then, falls into the category of policy for S&T. The study's report, *Rising Above the Gathering Storm: Energizing and Employing America for a Brighter Economic Future*,[6] focused on U.S. competitiveness in STEM fields. The report recommended that Congress:

- Increase America's talent pool by vastly improving K–12 mathematics and science education;
- Sustain and strengthen the nation's commitment to long-term basic research;
- Develop, recruit, and retain top students, scientists, and engineers from both the U.S. and abroad; and
- Ensure that the United States is the premier place in the world for innovation.

These recommendations are all related to the S&T enterprise, and so are "policy for S&T." This report led to the passage of the America COMPETES (Creating Opportunities to Meaningfully Promote Excellence in Technology, Education, and Science) Act.

So which category strikes you as most interesting? Inquiring minds want to know!

## What Is Policy Analysis?

When you are informing and influencing policymakers about your scientific and technical information, it is important that you take an evidence-based approach. Just as you would not make scientific and engineering decisions without analysis, the same is true with public policy.

That means that you take the time to research and analyze the different policy options rather than just "shooting from the hip" and recommending whatever policy option strikes your fancy. Too often, I see scientists, engineers, and health professionals make statements about a public policy issue without doing the appropriate analysis. Doing so reduces the credibility of the scientific and technical community. This is particularly true when focusing on a policy topic outside your scientific and technical expertise.

To develop an evidence-based policy position, you need to conduct a policy analysis. Policy analysis is a systematic process of analyzing potential policy options to respond to a societal problem and prioritizing those options based on their effectiveness, efficiency, equity, and ease of political acceptability. When policy analysis is conducted, the policy options identified are often oriented toward a particular client and their social values. A public policy option appropriate for the governor of California may differ from that for the governor of West Virginia.

Policy analysis is advice, not a direction to take action. Depending on the norms of the organization you work for, you may only present policy options, or you may make recommendations. For example, when I worked for the Congressional Research Service, a think tank for Congress, our analysis had to be extremely neutral and provided options without any bias toward which one to choose. This is because the viewpoints of members of Congress are multifaceted, and no one client was being served by that analysis. On the other hand, when I worked for the President's Council of Advisors on Science and Technology in the Obama Administration, the advice was for one person: President Obama. Our analysis took into account his norms as illustrated during the campaign and his decisions as president, and made recommendations accordingly.

Policymakers recognize that policy analysis may be biased, particularly when provided by interest groups. They may still find a biased analysis beneficial, because they often lack the detailed technical knowledge necessary to make the best decision. For policy analysis to be useful, first and foremost, it must be timely and provided prior to key decision-making points.

## What Happens If Policies Are Implemented without Analysis?

Without policy analysis, your chances of reaching the societal goal are less as you are making decisions without evidence. It's like deciding what college to go to or what house or car to buy without conducting any research to enhance your decision-making.

One example is the concept of microcredit. Its theory of change was that by making small investments in new or existing businesses, those businesses would increase their sales and profits. This in turn would increase household income, saving, and spending—resulting in improved health, education, and women's empowerment. In reality, though, scientific studies found that although the funding increased freedom in people's financial decisions and had no widespread harmful impact, it did not increase income, women's empowerment, or children's schooling.[7] More rigorous analysis prior to the widespread implementation of microcredit programs might have saved time and resources for policies that could have had a better chance of reaching these societal goals. Now that analysis has been completed, researchers have identified innovations that can help donors reach their societal goals with this mechanism.

Sometimes, too, a policy works as expected, but has unintentional side effects that lead to adverse consequences. China, for example, had a one-child policy where families could only have one child. The theory of change was that by reducing the country's population, economic growth would increase. The impact on China's society was dramatic—forced sterilizations, abortions, and infanticide. The policy was, however, "beneficial in terms of curbing population growth, aiding economic growth, and improving the health and welfare of women and children."[8] The policy ended in 2015, after 30 years, with the country in a demographic crisis due to too few young people supporting too many old people. There were also too many men, due to families preferring to have boys rather than girls as their single child, making it challenging to renew the population.[9]

## What Are the Steps in Policy Analysis?

There are many ways to approach public policy analysis. Here is my "recipe" based on my real-world experiences teaching policy analysis to scientists, engineers, and health professionals for several decades.[10]

## What Is Science and Technology Policy?

| Science and Technology Policy Analysis Steps | |
|---|---|
| Step 1: | Describe the societal problem. |
| Step 2: | Develop your "what actions, if any," policy question. |
| Step 3: | Identify two policy options in addition to the status quo. |
| Step 4: | Analyze the effectiveness of the status quo and the policy options. |
| Step 5: | Analyze the efficiency of the status quo and the policy options. |
| Step 6: | Analyze the equity of the status quo and the policy options. |
| Step 7: | Analyze the ease of political acceptability of the status quo and the policy options. |
| Step 8: | Synthesize the results of the 4E analysis. |
| Step 9: | Decide what policy option(s) to present or recommend. |
| Step 10: | Communicate the results of your analysis. |

In the following chapters, we'll go through each part of the process. For now, I'd like to provide an overview of the 4Es to you because they are at the heart of policy analysis.

## The 4Es: Effectiveness, Efficiency, Equity, & Ease of Political Acceptability

My first car, like that of many college students, was a hand-me-down from my parents—a big Oldsmobile with a powerful engine and lots of room to transport myself and my belongings from Texas to California. Yes, it was a gas-guzzler, and I was polluting the environment, but who was I to complain? It was free, and I only had to pay for the gas. I was living in Southern California, ironically pursuing my degree in mechanical and environmental engineering at the University of California, Irvine. But I was poor so I waved aside that contradiction.

Then the 1979 oil crisis hit. Thanks to a decrease in oil production during the Iranian revolution, gasoline suddenly required hours-long waits at gas stations when you could find it, and the prices soared as well. Suddenly my free gas-guzzler didn't look so effective in getting me from point A to point B. To save money, I tried the public transportation system, but it turned out to be two hours each way from where I was living to campus.

Now I had to make a decision. Should I stay with my current situation, living far from campus and waiting long hours for gas (the status quo), or should I change my plan? My goal: get to my classes on time. One option was to move closer to campus. Another option was to stay where I was and take a bus. Both would be effective in getting me to class.

In weighing my options, I had to consider several criteria. One was economic efficiency. Housing closer to campus was more expensive. On the other hand, I would have access to alternative transportation methods like walking and biking to get to my classes, which would counteract that expense. Another was equity—I would feel less guilty about polluting the environment. The last was the ease of political acceptability. Although I wouldn't use my car for commuting, my carless friends and I could still take it to the beach on the weekends—so I was sure I could convince them that moving was the right choice.

The other option, taking the bus, did not fare well in my analysis. Yes, housing would continue to be inexpensive, but time is money, and as an engineering student who also worked a part-time job, it was not economically efficient to add four hours' worth of commute time to my already packed daily schedule. I would still have the equity component because I was taking a bus, but buses still pollute more than walking or biking. And as for ease of political acceptability, I would be living closer to my friends so we could go to the beach more often. On the other hand, I would not be able to support my nondriving older relative who needed help with getting groceries, going to medical appointments, and other needs.

Policymakers are no different: when they make decisions, they weigh a variety of factors. So why, in our scientific and technical analysis, do we focus solely or primarily on effectiveness without considering any of these other factors? The purpose of this book is to help you develop a policy mindset to complement your science and technology mindset, so you know how to provide information on each of the 4Es[11] in your communication. The 4Es are:

### Effectiveness
- The degree to which a societal goal is more likely to be reached by implementing a policy.

### Efficiency:
- The cost of implementing the policy relative to its effectiveness. What policy gets the best bang for the societal buck?

### Equity:
- The fairness of the policy. Who are the winners and losers?

### Ease of political acceptability:
- The degree to which the policy is opposed or supported by key stakeholders. How likely is the policy to move forward in the political arena?

## What Is Science and Technology Policy?

So let's apply the 4E concept to my dilemma above. My suspicion is that you have made many similar decisions in your life as well and used similar criteria. It could be where you live, where you go to college, what kind of car to buy, and all the many other personal decisions you make every day. Here are some simple pro/con charts that incorporate the 4E concept. They are very similar to what you'll be doing when you get to steps 4–7 in the policy analysis process.

| 1: Long-Distance Commuting | Pro | Con |
|---|---|---|
| Effectiveness | Able to get to college in a reasonable time before the energy crisis | Reduced engagement in campus life and extracurricular activities |
| Efficiency | Lower housing and food costs | Higher transportation costs |
| Equity | Support nearby relatives who were unable to drive | Increase in my environmental impact on society |
| Ease of Political Acceptability | Objections of relatives who needed my help | Objections of my on-campus friends about my environmental impact |

| 2: Living on or near Campus | Pro | Con |
|---|---|---|
| Effectiveness | Reliable and easy access to campus for classes and extracurricular activities, enhancing my academic and social quality of life | On-campus living possibly less effective when I require a quieter, more controlled environment for studying |
| Efficiency | Higher housing and food costs, less time commuting | Lower transportation costs |
| Equity | Decrease in my environmental impact on society | Challenging to support relatives who are unable to drive |
| Ease of Political Acceptability | Objections of my on-campus friends about my environmental impact | Objections of relatives who needed my help |

## Developing Your Own Policy Analysis

As we move forward through the policy analysis process, you'll find that the analytical skills you have developed as a scientist, engineer, or health professional will serve you well. You know how to do literature searches, prepare research plans, conduct research, write summaries of findings, and develop conclusions based on those findings. The key is just learning about the analytical options that are available to you when you're in a public policy context.

> The best way to learn is by doing, not just reading. So throughout this book, you'll find "thought exercises" such as the one on the following page. I suggest you create a document that includes each exercise and your reflection on it. In the end, you'll hopefully see how you've evolved toward gaining a "policy mindset" that will serve you well in applying your scientific or technical skills to just about any societal problem.

If you visit the Science and Technology Policy Academy website (www.scitechpolicyacademy.com), you can obtain a free fillable PDF of the book, which you can use for all the thought exercises.

## What Is Science and Technology Policy?

### Thought Exercise 1: How Do You Make Decisions?

1. Are you interested in "policy for S&T" or "S&T for policy"?

   _____
   _____
   _____
   _____

2. Identify an example of an unsuccessful public policy. What went wrong?

   _____
   _____
   _____
   _____

3. Think about a decision you've made in your personal life. How did you make that decision? What criteria did you use? Was it something similar to the 4Es?

   _____
   _____
   _____
   _____

# Chapter 2
## Step 1: Describe the Societal Problem

Sometimes societal problems are long-term issues like climate change, hunger, drinking water quality, and healthcare equity. In other cases, societal problems arise because of the actions of others, and we need to develop a response to them.

The latter is where I had my first interaction with public policy analysis. Once I landed my first job as an engineer in Beaumont, Texas, I began volunteering for the League of Women Voters in Beaumont. (As an aside, volunteer experiences like these are a great way for you to gain experience in public policy.)

The league sent me to gather information on the ecological harm that might be caused by *Vulcanus*, a ship that wanted to anchor in the Gulf of Mexico and burn hazardous material. My job was to gather scientific and technical information, working to identify the hazards the vessel might pose and identify appropriate policies.

The league then developed positions based on my findings, through a consensus of its members. The process—gathering information from scientific and technical literature, presenting that to the members of the league, and then developing a position—was not that different from my later work in Washington, DC, developing consensus from committees of experts. In this case, though, there was hardly any scientific or technical literature to draw on. The league's policy recommendation was for more research to be done before *Vulcanus* was allowed to operate. Eventually, public opposition lead to *Vulcanus*'s activities being banned in an international agreement.

This is a good example of how you might identify a public policy topic where your scientific and technical analysis can play a role. It might be a long-term issue, or it might be an action that a policymaker or other organization proposes or has taken where you want to take action.

In this chapter, we're going to begin our journey into public policy analysis. We'll start with the first step of your policy analysis process: defining the societal problem you're going to address. The societal problems that we are focusing on in policy analysis are those in the "public interest," as described by President Abraham Lincoln in 1854:

# Step 1: Describe the Societal Problem

*The legitimate object of government, is to do for a community of people, whatever they need to have done, but can not do, at all, or can not, so well do, for themselves—in their separate, and individual capacities.*[12]

Science and technology policy analysis focuses on the interface between science and technology and public interest. This is clear in "S&T for policy," but even in the case of "policy for S&T," where benefits may go to the research community, the argument for that investment is for the resulting research that will generate benefits that will accrue to society.

## Identifying a Manageable Societal Problem for Your Policy Analysis

Here is a set of questions to start with to identify a concrete, manageable aspect of the societal problem of interest to you, followed by some guidance on each:

1. What societal problem are you trying to solve?
2. What are the root causes of the societal problem, according to stakeholders?
3. What are possible solutions to the societal problem, according to stakeholders?
4. Where might analysis play a role in developing the optimal policy to mitigate those root causes?
5. What is the geographic focus of your analysis?
6. What policymakers are the best focus for your analysis?
7. Are there any upcoming policy activities that are particularly relevant for your analysis?

### What Societal Problem Are You Trying to Solve?

The societal problem for our analysis can't be too large. The issue of how to help all people who don't have enough food (i.e., food insecurity), for instance, is too big to tackle in this case. You're going to need to limit your population to a manageable component. For example, helping the food insecure in urban areas is very different from helping those in rural areas. In addition, you need to incorporate current policies, which tend to be quite narrow. You also want to help those in most need based on the data available. In the table on page 22, you'll see we focused on "Households with children headed by a single woman have the highest rate of food insecurity," based on the available data. Note how narrow this population is.

## What Are the Root Causes of the Societal Problem, According to Stakeholders?

Our next step is to identify the root causes of why this particular population has high insecurity.

- "Root causes" are the fundamental, underlying issues or factors that lead to a particular societal problem or set of problems. If possible, you want to identify and address these root causes so you are addressing the problem at its source rather than simply treating the symptoms. You've probably heard something like this in the proverb: Give a man a fish, and you feed him for a day. Teach a man to fish, and you feed him for a lifetime. These are economic, social, political, environmental, technical, or institutional factors.

- "Stakeholders" are individuals, groups, or organizations directly or indirectly affected by the policy. Engaging with a diverse range of stakeholders is essential for a comprehensive understanding of the societal problem.

In our food insecurity example, available information from stakeholders indicates the root causes are race, education, incarceration, family income, jobs and networks, and neighborhoods.

## What Are Possible Solutions to the Societal Problem, According to Stakeholders?

Engaging with stakeholders is also important in identifying possible solutions to the societal challenge. The best experts on how to identify options for solving a problem are the people who are experiencing the challenge. Their solutions may not be perfect, but the same is true of you as an analyst. In our food insecurity example, the White House had a conference that brought many stakeholders together. This group identified the following solutions:

- Improve food access and affordability.
- Integrate nutrition and health.
- Empower all consumers to make and have access to healthy choices.
- Support physical activity for all.
- Enhance nutrition and food security research.

### Where Might Analysis Play a Role in Developing the Optimal Policy to Mitigate Those Root Causes?

Some policy decisions are totally political and analysis does not play a role, so you want to focus on decisions where a better understanding can lead to improved outcomes for those impacted by the societal challenge. Experts, particularly those from interest groups advocating for change, can often provide guidance as to where analysis would be useful for them. In our food insecurity case, those participating in the White House conference indicated that more analysis was needed on assessing equity within the federal nutrition assistance programs.

### What Is the Geographic Focus of Your Analysis?

The geographic focus is very important for policy analysis. A solution that might work well in one geographic region might not work well in another. The stakeholders can be very different, as are the root causes. In the food insecurity example, we are focusing on the United States. Think how different the analysis would be in India, Costa Rica, or Iceland and you'll see what I mean. The same is often true for states or even cities and counties within the same state.

### What Policymakers Are the Best Focus for Your Analysis?

Policymakers are those who decide whether to take action to respond to a societal problem. Government policymakers develop public policy. They include not only elected public officials at the national, state, and local levels, but also school boards, planning commissions, and an array of other decision-makers. They can also include those appointed by political leaders and civil servants, such as regulators or administrators in a public agency.

Policymakers, however, are not just those in government, but also individuals in nonprofit organizations, universities, foundations, businesses, and industries who make decisions that impact society. These people are making private policy.

For example, many firms have decided to proactively take action on climate change without any government requirement. For example, "Apple has been carbon neutral for its global corporate operations since 2020, and is laser-focused on its ambitious goal to become carbon neutral across its entire global supply chain and the life cycle of every product."[13]

Foundations, states, and nonprofit organizations can also decide to fund research on topics that the federal government is unwilling to fund or that they believe have insufficient funding. A good example is AmfAR, a foundation to fund AIDS research established in the early 1980s. Another example is stem cell research funded by voters through a California proposition that led to the establishment of the California Institute for Regenerative Medicine in 2004.[14]

Universities also make policies that focus on societal good. Some colleges and universities do not require tuition for low-income students, for example, or those from specific populations. Both Harvard and Stanford do not require tuition, room, or board for families whose income is less than $85,000 per year at Harvard[15] and $100,000 per year at Stanford.[16] Universities also make decisions regarding the diversity of their populations, the number of out-of-state or international students they accept, and free access to public transportation for students and faculty who live off campus.

So when you answer this question, think about who are the policymakers that are likely to have the most impact on the societal challenge. They may or may not be in government.

In our food insecurity example, however, we are focusing on government decision-makers. It is not sufficient, however, to say the president, Congress, or the federal government. You need to drill down to who will be making the decision. In this case, it is the administrator of the U.S. Department of Agriculture Food and Nutrition Service (FNS).

## Step 1: Describe the Societal Problem

### Are There Any Upcoming Relevant Policy Activities?

You want to understand the key points where your analysis might be able to best inform policymakers. Your analysis does not serve any purpose if you provide it a month after the decision is made. Policymakers won't go back and say, "Thank you so much for this analysis! We'll go back and change the policy we just approved!" So you need to find out what are the key policy activities so you can time your analysis. In our food insecurity case, it is the reauthorization of the farm bill.

### Food Insecurity Example

Food insecurity will be a running example that we will use to illustrate each step of the process. The lack of access to food is one of the oldest societal challenges that has faced the United States and is, of course, a challenge worldwide. The S&T policy community is constantly bringing data to the table to respond to this challenge, yet more still needs to be done, given that about 25% of American adults are considered food insecure.[17] Furthermore, more than nine million children (one in eight) in the United States are food insecure, including 22% of Black and 18.5% of Latino children due to structural inequities.[18]

This is both a long-standing issue and also one where events—such as the pandemic, economic conditions, and conflicts—can exacerbate the problem, leading to the need for new and revised policies. It is also one where all sorts of science and technology can play a role in responding to this societal challenge. Therefore, I think this is a good example to use for this book.

The table seen below shows the food insecurity example that we have described. Note that in the responses to each question, there is a citation to where that information came from. For evidence-based analysis, it is extremely important that you identify and work with the available data rather than any preconceived notions you might have. Often, you'll find that your perspective is incorrect or outdated.

On the other hand, finding data can often be challenging. If no quantitative data is available, you might need to gather qualitative data from stakeholders and experts in the field to gain a better understanding of the societal problem and its possible solutions.

From Expertise to Impact

In general, I recommend going through all the steps in the process based on a quick search initially just to help you better frame the societal problem. You can then start over, at a slower pace, and take the time you need to produce a quality analysis relative to your particular circumstances.

| Question | Response |
| --- | --- |
| 1. What societal problem are you trying to solve? | Households with children headed by a single woman have the highest rate of food insecurity.[19] |
| 2. What are the root causes of the societal problem, according to stakeholders? | Race, education, incarceration, family income, jobs and networks, neighborhoods[20] |
| 3. What are possible solutions to the societal problem, according to stakeholders? | Improve food access and affordability; integrate nutrition and health; empower all consumers to make and have access to healthy choices; support physical activity for all; enhance nutrition and food security research[21] |
| 4. Where might analysis play a role in developing the optimal policy to mitigate those root causes? | Assess equity within federal nutrition assistance programs[22] |
| 5. What is the geographic focus of your analysis? | United States |
| 6. What policymakers are the best focus for your analysis? | Administrator, U.S. Department of Agriculture Food and Nutrition Service (FNS) |
| 7. Are there any upcoming policy activities that are particularly relevant for your analysis? | Farm Bill reauthorization; Title IV: Nutrition accounts for 76% of Farm Bill expenditures. |

## Step 1: Describe the Societal Problem

Once we develop the answers to these questions, we need to confirm that the problem is limited in scope so it is possible to develop a solution within our time constraints efficiently. In some cases, our time frame is very limited. This may be because the societal problem is urgent, like the COVID epidemic, or because policy action is forthcoming. In the example above, the Farm Bill is coming up for reauthorization, and this is our best policy opportunity to address the issue of concern.

### Tip: Narrow Your Policy Focus

Almost all my students initially try to take on too big a problem. Just like scientific, engineering, and medical fields are broken down into disciplines, subdisciplines, and even sub-subdisciplines, the same is true for policy. Just as you wouldn't do a scientific paper on all of biology or physics, you shouldn't try to tackle a large, complex societal issue all at once. For example, climate change is a tremendously large issue, and to have an impact you need to focus on the unique contribution you can make in one particular niche. And, just as with scientific papers, you don't stop after one project. Over time you will build up a series of analyses in your policy niche.

From Expertise to Impact

## Thought Exercise 2: Societal Challenge of Interest to You

What is a societal challenge you want to use your scientific and technical knowledge to inform and influence policymakers and the public? Answer the following questions about it:

1. **What societal problem are you trying to solve?**

   _____
   _____
   _____
   _____
   _____
   _____

2. **What are the root causes of the societal problem, according to stakeholders?**

   _____
   _____
   _____
   _____
   _____
   _____

## Step 1: Describe the Societal Problem

**3. What are possible solutions to the societal problem, according to stakeholders?**

_____

_____

_____

_____

**4. Where might analysis play a role in developing the optimal policy to mitigate those root causes?**

_____

_____

_____

_____

**5. What is the geographic focus of your analysis?**

_____

_____

_____

_____

6. **What policymakers are the best focus for your analysis?**

_____

_____

_____

_____

_____


7. **Are there any upcoming policy activities that are particularly relevant for your analysis?**

_____

_____

_____

_____

_____

# Chapter 3

## Step 2: Develop Your "What Actions, If Any" Policy Question

The biggest challenge in any science and technology policy analysis is definitely breaking down the societal problem you want to address into a policy question that is feasible for your analysis and where you can make a unique contribution. Breaking down the problem takes more time than you might expect. Albert Einstein once said, "If I had an hour to solve a problem, I'd spend 55 minutes thinking about the problem and 5 minutes thinking about solutions" (attributed).

Once the problem is clearly defined, the actual analysis is much easier.

### Challenges in Developing Your S&T Policy Analysis

I've taught science and technology policy analysis to thousands of people over the years. Without a doubt, regardless of whether they are a junior or senior scientist or engineer, step 2 is the hardest challenge they face in the process.

Here's the challenge people typically face:

- **They want to solve the entire problem**—say climate change—but there are so many ways to address this challenge that it's too big for any one policy analysis. Try to think of it like you would a science or engineering challenge. You don't come up with a cure for cancer through one scientific paper. Instead, hundreds if not thousands of individual analyses may contribute to the actions that are eventually taken.

- **They don't recognize there is an existing policy (the status quo).** There is always some policy in place now. So let's say you're a fan of electric vehicles and that's where you want to focus your analysis. You need to recognize that there are existing policies out there at the federal level and sometimes even at the state and local levels. So you will need to take that into account when developing your question. What niche will you address where policy analysis will be useful? For example, you might want to think about possible policies that address equity issues associated with the purchase or charging of electric vehicles.

- **They don't take into account the geographic region.** They might, for example, be interested in STEM education. In the United States, however, STEM education is not managed at the national level but at the state and local levels. In addition, each community has different human and economic resources. The issue is not just rich and poor, but also urban versus rural, and those who do or do not have internet access. So the policy question can differ a great deal depending on what the current situation is for a very localized geographic region.

- **They don't take into account the policymaker's jurisdiction.** You might think that the administrator of the Environmental Protection Agency has jurisdiction over all environmental policies in the United States. They don't. There is certainly a minimum environmental policy, but states and local communities can implement stricter policies. California, for example, has much stricter environmental laws than the rest of the United States because of its particular challenges. You also saw jurisdictional conflicts during the pandemic when some state governors wanted weaker policies on masking than the mayors of cities within their state. The governors could not dictate city policy, and the mayors could not dictate state policy because each lacked jurisdiction over the other on this issue.

For these reasons, I developed the following model. By using this model you can avoid many of these challenges at the start, saving you a great deal of time later in the policy analysis process.

## Policy Question Model: "What Actions, If Any"

After gathering your thoughts on the focus of your analysis, your next step is to put them in the form of what I call the "What actions, if any" policy question, as shown here. The goal of this step is to make it clear what question you are trying to answer in your analysis and provide the specificity necessary to make developing the answer manageable.

## Step 2: Develop Your "What Actions, If Any" Policy Question

*What actions, if any, should POLICYMAKER take to respond to concerns about SOCIETAL PROBLEM in GEOGRAPHIC REGION?*

Here's the thought behind each element of the question. Your goal is to fill out the information in all caps and keep the rest of the question the same.

1. **"If any"** helps to make sure you do not presume a policy action will take place. One common mistake students make when conducting policy analysis is not acknowledging that there is a current policy out there (the "status quo") addressing the societal problem. They tend to immediately move to the actions they think should occur. Realistically, however, on most issues no additional action is taken, either because the status quo is genuinely the best option or because the analyst didn't make a strong enough case to justify that the benefits of a new measure outweigh its costs.

2. **"Policymaker"** makes clear which policymaker you are addressing. Each policymaker has a different jurisdiction and the policies they can implement. The governor of Virginia doesn't make policy for Kansas. Policies that work well in one region may not work well in another region. Even the president and Congress don't have jurisdiction over all policies in the United States.

3. **"Respond to concerns"** is part of the question to remind you to offer rigorous proof that there is a societal problem, and how bad that problem is, as part of your analysis.

4. **"Societal problem"** is included so you clearly describe what specific societal problem you are addressing. In order to assess the effectiveness of your possible policy options, you need to have some measure of how impactful policy options will be in responding to that problem.

5. **"Geographic region"** is important to include because a solution that works in one country, city, township, or school district may not work in another.

## Good Question

Here's an example of a good "What actions, if any," question:

> *What actions, if any, should Alberta's minister of Environment and Sustainable Resource Development take to respond to concerns that energy companies are not taking sufficient action to reduce their greenhouse gas emissions from oil sands in Alberta?*

- "If any" indicates that no additional action is presumed. In Alberta, for example, they already have a carbon tax. So the question is whether that tax is a sufficient disincentive to polluters. In other provinces there is no tax on companies, but there is on mobile sources of greenhouse gas. Is that approach more or less effective?

- "Alberta's Minister" refers to an individual who can take action.

- "Energy companies" shows that there is specificity about the sources involved. (For example, mobile sources are not included.)

- "Greenhouse," "oil sands," and "Alberta" all provide additional specificity about which pollutants from what source in what location.

## Bad Question

Here's an example of a bad "What actions, if any" question. Before you continue reading, try to figure out on your own why it is not a good question:

> *What actions, if any, should be taken by the National Oceanic and Atmospheric Administration (NOAA) to encourage fisheries to reduce wasted catch?*

- "NOAA" indicates the challenge of addressing all of NOAA as your policymaker because it is a big organization. When an organization is this large, there is no accountability when you make your policy recommendations—who

## Step 2: Develop Your "What Actions, If Any" Policy Question

are you even sending your emails to? The more specificity you can provide, the better. In this case we should add the "Assistant Administrator for Fisheries," who holds direct responsibility for this issue.

- "Encourage" implies that some sort of incentive system will be used, as opposed to alternatives like regulation or voluntary mechanisms. You don't want your question to be assuming a particular solution yet; before you start your analysis you need to be open to all possibilities.

- "Fisheries" brings up the idea that NOAA only has jurisdiction over ocean fisheries.[23] There are fisheries in the interior of the United States, managed by regional councils, and of course fisheries that are outside of areas where the United States has legal authority. So not only is more specificity needed on the kind of fisheries, but also we need a geographic location.

- "Wasted catch" is jargon that must be defined. What "wasted catch" means to me may be different from what it means to you. So more specificity is needed to make clear the issue at hand. A related problem is that the phrase "respond to concerns" is missing, which means you haven't established that wasted catch is even a problem. The problem we are trying to solve is unclear, and this makes it challenging to access the effectiveness of our policy options because we don't know the status quo.

**Here's a possible revision:**

*What actions, if any, should the Assistant Administrator for Fisheries at National Oceanic and Atmospheric Administration (NOAA) take to respond to concerns that an excessive number of sea turtles die because they are caught in shrimping nets in U.S. ocean fisheries?*[24]

Compared to the first version, this question is neutral, so it does not assume there is a problem, yet it provides enough specificity that the status quo and alternative policy options can be assessed on their potential effectiveness.

## Food Insecurity Example

Now let's go back to our question about hunger from the table we put together in the previous section:

> *What actions, if any, should the administrator at the U.S. Department of Agriculture Food and Nutrition Service (FNS) take to respond to equity concerns about federal nutrition assistance programs, particularly for households with children headed by a single woman that have the highest rate of food insecurity in the United States?*

This question makes it clear which population with food insecurity we are focusing upon in our analysis. Obviously, the other populations are of concern as well, and some will overlap with the population in the question, but the policies for this population may need to be different. Understanding the barriers faced by that specific population leading to the higher rate of food insecurity will help identify the policy solutions that will work with their lifestyle and needs.

## Tip: Get Feedback on Your Question

Peer feedback is a very important part of the policy analysis process, just like it is for any other part of the scientific and technical enterprise. Your question will be improved if you discuss it with others. Just the act of explaining the question and getting other thoughts on it will help in your own thinking. It's also good to talk to experts, stakeholders, and nonexperts because each will provide a different perspective. For example, a common challenge is that you are using jargon that a nonexpert has no idea what it means. This will reduce the ultimate clarity of your analysis.

Think about how you can get this peer feedback at each stage of the policy analysis process. Having an accountability buddy, with each of you working on your own analysis, is also a great way both to get feedback and to encourage progress on your analysis.

Step 2: Develop Your "What Actions, If Any" Policy Question

## Thought Exercise 3: Develop Your "What Actions, If Any" Policy Question

Use the following model to develop your policy question that you will use as a basis for the thought exercises throughout the rest of this book. Keep in mind that as you learn more, you can go back and modify the question. So it doesn't have to be perfect, but you need a good starting point:

1. **What actions, if any, should POLICYMAKER take to respond to concerns about SOCIETAL PROBLEM in GEOGRAPHIC REGION?**

_____

_____

_____

_____

_____

_____

_____

# Chapter 4

## Step 3: Identify Two Policy Options in Addition to the Status Quo

When I was working on that first study at NASEM related to climate change, one of the committee members was a man named Robert Frosch, the first assistant executive director for the UN Environment Programme, a former NASA administrator, and vice president of research at General Motors at the time of the study. In one of many enlightening casual conversations I had with members during the committee dinners, Dr. Frosch asked for my thoughts about a policy option that was definitely "unthinkable" to me at the time. It was about the question of why we don't require that everyone live in apartments instead of single-family houses. I was always the youngest person at these dinners, living in an apartment at the time but aspiring someday to have a single-family home, primarily so I could easily support having a dog.

Realistically, from a climate perspective, the resources required by an apartment building are less than for a house, and there would be fewer greenhouse gas emissions as a result. Yet the American dream is to own a house. Buying a house is often the biggest investment a family ever makes. So the policy, while effective and efficient, would certainly face some challenges in ease of political acceptability and equity. But it was still worth bringing up! Treating certain climate solutions as "unthinkable" rather than merely radical had made it harder for me and my fellow committee members to be creative and investigate all avenues.

Dr. Frosch also suggested analysis of other "out-of-the-box" options in the report, like mirrors in space, seeding the ocean with iron, and putting particulates into the atmosphere—all in an effort to cool down the earth. These were "unthinkable" at the time, but today we are seriously considering some of these options because of the decades of research initiated at that time. If nations can't reduce greenhouse gas emissions quickly enough, these policy options may become particularly relevant.

Those conversations led me to recognize that I shouldn't just repeat the same policies others promoted. Instead, I needed to "think out of the box" and encourage others to do the same. Brainstorming what can seem to be wacky ideas can actually result in unique solutions when policymakers and the S&T community are "stuck" in the same mode of thinking.

# Step 3: Identify Two Policy Options in Addition to the Status Quo

So in step 3, where you identify the policy options, identify two policy options—alternative courses of action to the status quo—and try to go beyond your personal preferences and biases. Explore the many policy options that have been proposed and identify or consider "out-of-the-box" policy options as well.

At the same time, an important consideration in developing policy options is understanding the specific jurisdiction that the targeted policymaker can influence. So you also need to think "inside the box" of what's possible given your narrowly defined area of focus.

This chapter will discuss ways to identify a list of policy options and then narrow that list down to the two specific options that you will analyze.

In identifying policy options, we need to take a number of steps. The first is to analyze the effectiveness of the current policy and gather the ideas of stakeholders about ways it could be adapted without scrapping it entirely. The second is to seek "parallel" policies—those that have been enacted in other jurisdictions—and see if they are worth considering. The third is to think "out of the box" and come up with entirely new options.

## Gather Stakeholder Opinions on the Status Quo

The first step in developing your policy options is to understand the status quo and stakeholder opinions on it. Here we need to answer four questions:

1. What is the current policy in place to respond to the societal challenge?

2. What works well in this program, according to stakeholders?

3. What does not work well in this program, according to stakeholders?

4. What are some of the other policies that have been proposed to respond to the societal challenge?

Ideally, to answer these questions, you will have a program evaluation to rely upon. A program evaluation is when an internal, external, or advisory committee assesses how well a program is working. Unfortunately, we don't always have a program evaluation, or the quality of that evaluation is questionable.

It's also important to incorporate the perspectives of stakeholders. The more input we are able to gather from stakeholders, the greater the credibility of our analysis. Here are some ways to gather stakeholder input if you are able to interact directly with stakeholders:

- Surveys
- Interviews
- Focus groups

When I'm gathering information from stakeholders, I use all three of the above techniques to gather both qualitative and quantitative data. Typically I'll ask the stakeholders to fill out a survey first to gather some demographic data and to get them thinking about the issues I want them to address. In general, I find people do not respond to surveys in a sufficiently substantive way to be useful for identifying policy options, so I need to add focus groups and interviews.

If it is the individuals being served by the program, I'll attempt to gather five to ten of them in a small focus group. For example, when I did a focus group with unemployed workers in Pittsburgh, I asked them to comment on each other's policy ideas to see if there was a consensus.

If it is instead an organization, I'll typically conduct personal interviews with leaders in that organization (virtually or in-person) to gather additional information. Similarly, I'll test out ideas from other organizations that are similar. For example, when speaking to manufacturing organizations, I'll share in an anonymous way the ideas and reflections from other manufacturers to see if there is some consensus on the ideas. I also share ideas or concerns from the potential employees (in this case the unemployed workers mentioned above.

If you cannot interact with the stakeholders directly, here are other options:

- Use Google News or similar sources to read articles and see what individual stakeholders say in response to a reporter's questions.

- Use Google, Google News, or similar sources to identify public interest organizations and think tanks that focus on your topic of interest.

    - Go to the organizations' websites and look for a specific page focused on public policy to see what they say about the program and what actions they are advocating.

Step 3: Identify Two Policy Options in Addition to the Status Quo

- These organizations can be at the international, national, state, or local level. You may need to modify their recommended policy so it is appropriate for your policymaker and geographic region.

- Use https://www.congress.gov/ managed by the Library of Congress, to see what policies have already been proposed by members of Congress, which probably were initially suggested to them by stakeholders.

    - Using this tool, you can search for your topic (e.g., electric vehicles) and see what policies have been proposed. If you're working at the national level, you can analyze these policies; most have probably been proposed without any analysis, so it can be useful for policymakers.

    - If you're at the state or local levels, consider that the most innovative policies in the United States typically start at that level and you can consider proposing one of the congressional-level policies for the geographic area that is the focus of your analysis.

## Identify Parallel Policies in Other Regions

Another way to come up with policy ideas is to see what is happening in other countries, states, and regions. This option has a number of advantages. First, you can review news articles from before a given policy was approved, to see who supported and opposed the proposal and what modifications were made as a result. Second, if the program has been in place for a number of years, there may be both qualitative and quantitative data that can be used to assess the 4Es for that option. Third, you will ideally be able to access data on how much the program costs in a real-world context.

So how do you find such policies? Here are some ideas:

- **Look for case studies on international, national, and local government websites.** These are typically profiles of somewhere in the world where a policy that addresses a societal need has worked sufficiently well to get visibility. For example, for our case study, I used the search terms "international hunger woman children" and then "public policy" in quotes. I found a United Nations World Food Programme report with a number of policy ideas, including take-home food from school lunch programs, support for kitchen gardens, and food-for-training programs.[25]

- **Look for nonprofit organizations that have an idea that might be worth replicating in a government setting.** Google News is a good way to find these organizations. In our food insecurity example, one idea that came up when I used the search term "best food insecurity programs" was a program in Canada called Mealshare. The way this program works is that when you buy a meal at a restaurant, you can donate a Mealshare menu item to a youth in need. Mealshare then receives funds from the restaurant, which are donated to partner organizations that feed youth.[26] You might have seen similar programs in the United States asking for a donation to your local food bank when you buy gas or groceries.

- **Look at global or state rankings and see what other countries and states are doing the best and look at their policies.** I looked at the Global Food Security Index for our example analysis and found two countries with the highest rankings: Finland and Ireland.[27] I decided to look at Ireland as it is a country with a well-known history of food insecurity that led some to migrate to the United States. Specific reasons cited for Ireland's high food security are food affordability (most food is grown locally) and higher-than-average funding for agriculture research and development (focused on reducing food loss).[28] Advocates are still pushing the envelope in Ireland, including proposing that taxes for locally grown food should be reduced or eliminated, as well as providing incentives for local food start-ups.[29]

When assessing these parallel policies, you want to answer this question:

- How similar is it to your situation? Ireland, for example, may or may not be a good illustration for your geographic reason. If not, you should discard this as an option and not move forward with the other questions.

The following questions should be answered to see if it's worthwhile to consider this idea as a policy option for your question:

- How effective is the current policy? What works? What doesn't work?
- How much does the current policy cost?

## Step 3: Identify Two Policy Options in Addition to the Status Quo

- Who does the current policy help? Who does the current policy hurt?
- Who supports the current policy? Who opposes the current policy?

This 4E analysis will help you decide whether to add the option to your list of policy option ideas that you will narrow down later.

### Develop and Seek "Out-of-the-Box" Policies

One of my favorite out-of-the-box ideas is the concept of the general public using the electric vehicle charging stations now being installed at U.S. post offices as the mail service moves to electric vehicles. Although not without challenges,[30] this might provide locations in both urban and rural communities for electric charging, support people traveling with a known charging location, and provide a source of revenue and a new mission for the post office in a changing world. A good existing illustration is the way public libraries now offer many more services than checking out books, like providing a place for the public to access the internet and 3D printing equipment.

Here are some ways to develop and seek out-of-the-box policy options for consideration:

- **Look for articles in Google News that might have more radical ideas.** For our food insecurity example, I used the same search terms as earlier and found an article that identifies a number of unique proposals. Among the proposals are forbidding speculation on agricultural futures, keeping agriculture out of free trade agreements, and forbidding the use of agriculture to provide agrofuel or energy.[31]

- **Brainstorm ideas with colleagues using a list of the policy mechanisms.** Although most people's minds tend to go to regulation and taxes when considering policies, there are a number of other options. The table seen below provides you with some ideas as a starting point. For our food insecurity example, one idea is to provide childcare to encourage single women with children to apply for the WIC program. This would fall in the "service provision" category.

- **Look for policy concepts that work for another social challenge.** In this case, I Googled and came across a policy brief from researchers in New

Zealand that discussed the U.S. Internal Revenue Service (IRS) program that used information on income to provide "nudges" to people to apply for a program for which they were eligible.[32]

| Policy Mechanism[33] | Brief Definition | Examples |
|---|---|---|
| Taxes | Mandatory financial charges | Carbon tax, research and development tax credit |
| Regulation | Rules governing conduct | Environmental regulation, Zero-Emission Vehicle (ZEV) program |
| Subsidies and Grants | Provide financial aid | Pell Grants for undergraduate education, research grants |
| Service Provision | Delivering public services | Public transportation, vaccination programs |
| Information | Providing necessary knowledge | Public health information, appliance and car energy efficiency labeling |
| The Structure of Private Rights | Defining legal entitlements | Intellectual property rights, civil rights |
| Education and Consultation | Learning and feedback | Public education, National Academies of Sciences, Engineering, and Medicine studies |
| Financing and Contracting | Funding and agreements | NASA and Space X, public-private healthcare partnership |
| Bureaucratic and Political Reforms | Improving governance systems | Establishment of the Environmental Protection Agency and the National Institutes of Health |

## Step 3: Identify Two Policy Options in Addition to the Status Quo

Here are some questions to help you decide whether you should add a policy idea to your list of possibilities:

- What government agency would implement the idea? Is it within the jurisdiction of your policymaker?

- Is there any evidence that the proposed policy might be effective? Or is it just an idea?

- Is there any information on how much the policy would cost to implement? If not, is there some way to estimate the cost?

- Who might the policy help? Harm?

- Who is likely to support or oppose the policy? How strong is that support or opposition?

### Picking Your Two Options for Analysis

Once you go through the process detailed above, the question then is how to narrow down these many options to identify the two that you will analyze in addition to the status quo. Based on what you know, consider the 4Es for each option. That should greatly narrow down the list of options.

Then ask yourself, if your preferred policy is such a good idea, why isn't it already in place? You might want to bring in family and friends to help if you can only see the pros for a policy idea and not the cons. In addition, you should make sure that the two options are sufficiently dissimilar from each other. If you think both should be chosen, merge those options together and pick another.

The reason I suggest limiting your analysis to two options is that you need to make sure your work is reasonable in terms of the time it will take and that it is of sufficient quality. In addition, policymakers can be overwhelmed if you give them too many choices. You might have felt this yourself, as I've given you all these ideas to identify possible policy options!

Always remember that less is more when it comes to public policy. Although your concept is of utmost importance to you, the policymaker to whom you are addressing it may have hundreds if not thousands of topics that they need to consider. Keep it simple.

## Food Insecurity Example

Let's try answering the questions outlined above for our food insecurity program using methods that do not require direct interaction with stakeholders. For the other methods, we've given examples throughout the discussion of each.

| Question | Response |
|---|---|
| 1. What societal problem are you trying to solve? | The Special Supplemental Nutrition Program for Women, Infants, and Children (WIC) helps pregnant women, mothers, and caregivers of infants and young children learn about good nutrition to keep themselves and their families healthy. On average, 6.2 million people participated in the WIC program with a $5.0 billion budget. Related programs include the National School Lunch Program (NSLP), School Breakfast Program (SBP), Child and Adult Care Food Program (CACFP), and the Summer Food Service Program (SFSP).[34] |
| 2. What are the root causes of the societal problem, according to stakeholders? | The Biden Administration announced plans in 2022 to dramatically expand access to and strengthen the WIC program.[35] Studies have found WIC is a "cost-effective investment that improves the nutrition and health of low-income families—leading to healthier infants, more nutritious diets and better healthcare for children, and subsequently to higher academic achievement for students."[36] |
| 3. What are possible solutions to the societal problem, according to stakeholders? | Only three out of five families eligible for the WIC program participate. Barriers include (1) misconceptions about eligibility; (2) transportation and other costs to reach WIC clinics; (3) language and clinical barriers; (4) negative clinical experiences (e.g., long wait times, poor customer service); (5) applying for services requires time away from work risking job loss and lost wages; (6) discontent with children's food packages; and (7) limited foods allowable for WIC resulting in embarrassing checkout experiences.[37] |

## Step 3: Identify Two Policy Options in Addition to the Status Quo

| | |
|---|---|
| **4. What are some of the policies that have been proposed to respond to the societal challenge?** | H.R.8450—The Healthy Meals, Healthy Kids Act would modernize the Special Supplemental Nutrition Program for Women, Infants, and Children (WIC) by requiring WIC clinics to offer services over the phone and via video options. It also allows remote benefit issuance and extends WIC benefits to children up to six years old, and extends certification periods to two years for infants, children, and postpartum individuals.<br><br>The S.853 / H.R.2011—Wise Investment in Children Act (WIC Act) would extend the WIC certification period to two years; extend eligibility for children from 5 years until their sixth birthday; and extend postpartum eligibility to two years for all mothers.[38] |

After looking at the current landscape, we're going to focus on the following two options. Why did I pick these? Primarily because they have a higher "ease of political acceptability" as they are already part of the legislative discussion, but perhaps just need analysis to better understand their effectiveness, efficiency, and equity. And for these 4Es, I believe there will be sufficient data available to assess each relative to the status quo. Even if there is not information specific to this circumstance, it should not be hard to develop estimates and make a reasonable judgment that will support evidence-based decision-making.

- Option 1: USDA's FNS should require WIC clinics to offer services over the phone and via video options and allow remote benefit issuance.

- Option 2: USDA's FNS should provide transportation vouchers to assist clients in going to WIC clinics.

### Tip: Go Beyond Your Own Policy Ideas

I hope you see the importance of conducting research in a variety of ways to come up with a wide array of policy options. I frequently see my students start with their own ideas based on what they know or have read, thinking that is all that is needed for them to move forward with their policy analysis. Once they begin to conduct the research, I suggest, however, they begin to see a much bigger universe of policy ideas than they anticipated.

From Expertise to Impact

## Thought Exercise 4: Identify Two Policy Options to Analyze

Using the methods in this chapter, make a list of potential policy options. Considering the 4Es, which two do you think are worth investigating further? Write them in a format similar to the following. Make sure you include both who would take the action (USDA's FNS in our examples) as well as the action itself. This is a common error.

- Option 1: USDA's FNS should require WIC clinics to offer services over the phone and via video options and allow remote benefit issuance.

- Option 2: USDA's FNS should provide transportation vouchers to assist clients in going to WIC clinics.

- **Option 1:**

_____

_____

_____

_____

- **Option 2:**

_____

_____

_____

_____

# Chapter 5
## Step 4: Analyze the Effectiveness of the Status Quo and the Policy Options

I love meeting scientists, engineers, and health professionals who care about making a difference in society—from young high school students to senior professionals. We hear far too much from the world's pessimists; it is wonderful to hear from the world's optimists instead.

When I was teaching energy policy, for example, I would ask students what was the most important action policymakers should take to reduce greenhouse gas emissions. Many students would choose switching to electric vehicles, because they emit no greenhouse gas emissions. And this is true—if you only look at tailpipe emissions or when the source of electricity is a renewable energy source like hydropower, solar, or wind energy. This represents the perspective of optimists.

From a pessimist standpoint, however, you also need to look at the source of the electricity in a given region. In the United States (and most countries in the world), most of that electricity still comes from fossil fuels (60% in 2021), and only 20% comes from renewable sources, with an additional 20% coming from nuclear energy (and many of these plants are closing). So, while electric vehicles can contribute to greenhouse gas mitigation, adopting them is not as effective as many of my students think unless it's combined with a massive switch to new energy sources.

So I encourage my students to analyze effectiveness for an array of options, take a systems perspective, and consider the geographic location of where their proposed policy is implemented. Little by little, as they read news articles that provide different perspectives from the academic setting and gather the data available from government websites, they gain the necessary policy mindset to realistically identify what policy options will be most effective in reaching the societal goal they care about.

Fundamentally, effectiveness is the most important "E" from my perspective, and why it should be the first you consider. If a policy option is not more effective than the status quo, then why implement it unless it provides the same amount of effectiveness at a lower cost (efficiency criteria) or helps disadvantaged populations (equity criteria)? In addition, occasionally students will assess the status quo and find that the current policy is effective. Why would a policymaker want to take on the challenging task of obtaining support for the new policy then? Again, only if it helped on the other 4E criteria.

## Develop a Logic Model for the Status Quo

Program evaluation is the process of understanding the effectiveness of a program—after you've identified your two options in step 3, it's time to analyze the potential effectiveness for the status quo and then compare your two options to the status quo to see the degree to which, if any, these options are likely to be more effective than the current policy in place.

Logic models are a graphical depiction of the "theory of action" between the resources, activities, outputs, and outcomes of a program. By developing a logic model for the status quo, you can:

- **Clarify the current program objectives, budget, resources, activities, and outcomes.** Sometimes the challenge is not with the design of the program but rather the lack of sufficient resources, or inappropriate allocation of those resources, to implement the program. On the other hand, if you propose a policy option that is double the existing budget, then its ease of political acceptability is low regardless of how effective it may be.

- **Identify the indicators used to measure the program's effectiveness currently.** These same indicators may or may not be useful in helping you see how well the program is meeting the goals in your question. For example, if your policy question is focused on equity and that is not measured, it will be hard to make a comparison of the new policies with the existing program without additional data collection. On the other hand, if it is measured, this is a good way to see how well the proposed policies compare to the status quo.

- **Provide a standard framework for policy option comparison.** I cannot tell you how many times I've met with a policymaker with an idea and they say, we're doing what you propose already. But in reality, they are not. However, if you don't have sufficient understanding of the current

Step 4: Analyze the Effectiveness of the Status Quo and the Policy Options

program and its degree of effectiveness, communicating with policymakers at the conclusion of your analysis is challenging and may result in them not implementing a better evidence-based policy option than is taking place today.

Here's an example of a simple logic model:

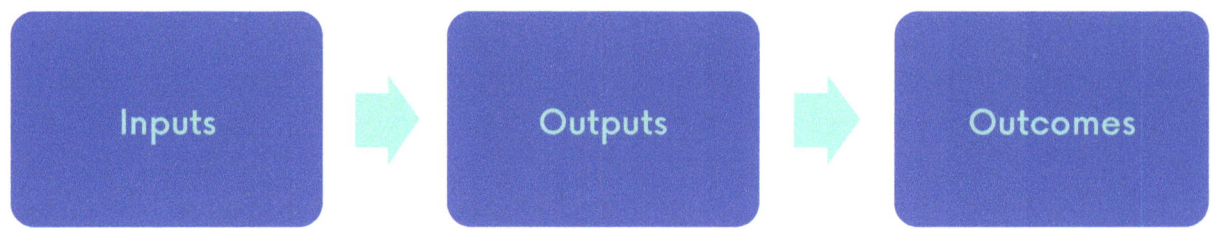

- Inputs are the resources put into a program. Typical examples are funding and staff.

- Outputs are the program activities and who participated in those activities.

- Outcomes are the societal changes that result from the program.

Together, these elements describe the "theory of action"—our hypothesis as to what will happen if the resources are put in place. Say, for example, that we are concerned about unemployed individuals in coal communities and are considering a program that would train these individuals to work in cybersecurity instead.

- The inputs are the financial resources, facilities, and people needed.

- The outputs are the coal community members who sign up and receive training in cybersecurity.

- The outcomes are the trained individuals who are able to get cybersecurity jobs—and not just any cybersecurity job. From a societal standpoint, we want them to get middle-class, family-supporting jobs that allow them to stay in their community and support its economy.

Now let's try this with our food insecurity example. As a reminder, here is our policy analysis question:

*What actions, if any, should the administrator at the U.S. Department of Agriculture Food and Nutrition Service (FNS) take to respond to equity concerns about federal nutrition assistance programs, particularly for households with children headed by a single woman, which have the highest rate of food insecurity in the United States?*

And here are our options:

- **Status quo:** The Special Supplemental Nutrition Program for Women, Infants, and Children (WIC) helps pregnant women, mothers, and caregivers of infants and young children learn about good nutrition to keep themselves and their families healthy. It provides nutrition services, breastfeeding support, healthcare, social service referrals, and healthy foods to eligible participants.

- **Option 1:** USDA's FNS should require WIC clinics to offer services over the phone and via video options and allow remote benefit issuance.

- **Option 2:** USDA's FNS should require WIC clinics to provide transportation vouchers to assist clients in going to WIC clinics.

The first step I typically take after choosing my options is to find an existing logic model to use as a base for my own assessment. In this case, I went to Google Images, used the search terms "logic model food insecurity children," and found a logic model from the Oregon State government.[39] That model is more complicated than we need for our assessment at this stage, so I developed the mini-version that you see here, focused on our "What actions, if any" question.

| Inputs | Outputs | Outcomes |
|---|---|---|
| • Community Health Workers<br>• WIC Funding<br>• Local Food Pantries<br>• School Meals<br>• Participation Data | • Participants: Pregnant and single women with children under 5<br>• Activities: Screen client eligibility, Increase access to healthy affordable food<br>• Process Measures: Percent of clients screened & provided with access to affordable, healthy food | • Short-term: Increased food security skills<br>• Mid-term: Empowered families with access to safe, healthy, and culturally acceptable food<br>• Long-term: Reduced risk of poor physical and mental health, developmental delays, growth problems, malnutrition |

## Step 4: Analyze the Effectiveness of the Status Quo and the Policy Options

We previously looked for an evaluation of the WIC program and found a number of barriers that were preventing single mothers from taking part. That evaluation found that the WIC program works well in reaching its goals with those who participate, but too few eligible women apply for the program.[40] One common challenge program staff face in conducting program evaluations is that they tend not to interact with the people who are not current participants.

So we will now update this standard logic model to specifically measure improvement in the challenge we are addressing—eligible women who are declining to participate in the WIC program. I've added an additional measure at the end of the outputs section and at the beginning of the outcomes section. They are highlighted with asterisks.

### Inputs
- Community Health Workers
- WIC Funding
- Local Food Pantries
- School Meals
- Participation Data

### Outputs
- Participants: Pregnant and single women with children under 5
- Activities: Screen client eligibility, Increase access to healthy affordable food
- Process Measures: Percent of clients screened & provided with access to affordable, healthy food
- **Percent of eligible women who decline to participate in the program.**

### Outcomes
- Short-term: Increased food security skills **for women who declined to participate in the program previously**
- Mid-term: Empowered families with access to safe, healthy, and culturally acceptable food
- Long-term: Reduced risk of poor physical and mental health, developmental delays, growth, malnutrition

### Modify the Status Quo Logic Model with Policy Option Activities

Our next step is to modify this logic model with our policy options. What we are setting up is a before-and-after model. So we will measure the percentage of eligible women who are not applying for the program before each intervention, and then see if the percentage increases after the intervention. Typically, this measurement would be done via a pilot program in one community. If that works, we would then expand it to additional communities.

From Expertise to Impact

**Option 1:** USDA's FNS should require WIC clinics to offer services over the phone and via video options and allow remote benefit issuance. (*** indicate changes in original logic model)

### Inputs
- Community Health Workers Available in Office
- ***Community Health Workers Available via Phone and Video***
- WIC Funding
- Local Food Pantries
- School Meals
- Participation Data

### Outputs
- Participants: Pregnant and single women with children under 5
- Activities: Screen client eligibility, Increase access to healthy affordable food
- ***Phone/Video Assistance***
- Process Measures: Percent of clients screened & provided with access to affordable, healthy food
- **Percent of eligible women who decline to participate in the program.**

### Outcomes
- Short-term: Increased food security skills **for women who declined to participate in the program previously**
- Mid-term: ***More*** Empowered families with access to safe, healthy, and culturally acceptable food
- Long-term: ***Increase in children that have a*** Reduced risk of poor physical and mental health, developmental delays, growth, malnutrition

**Option 2:** USDA's FNS should provide transportation vouchers to assist clients in going to WIC clinics. (*** indicate changes in original logic model)

### Inputs
- Community Health Workers
- WIC Funding
- Local Food Pantries
- School Meals
- Participation Data
- ***Drivers transporting women and children to clinics***

### Outputs
- Participants: Pregnant and single women with children under 5
- Activities: Screen client eligibility, Increase access to healthy affordable food
- ***Transportation to clinic assistance***
- Process Measures: Percent of clients screened & provided with access to affordable, healthy food
- **Percent of eligible women who decline to participate in the program.**

### Outcomes
- Short-term: Increased food security skills **for women who declined to participate in the program previously***
- Mid-term: ***More*** Empowered families with access to safe, healthy, and culturally acceptable food
- Long-term: ***Increase in children who have a*** Reduced risk of poor physical and mental health, developmental delays, growth, malnutrition

## Step 4: Analyze the Effectiveness of the Status Quo and the Policy Options

Now that we have our model set up, before we actually try to institute pilot programs, let's move to a pro/con analysis of the effectiveness of these two options.

### Develop a Pro/Con Effectiveness Analysis of Status Quo and Policy Options

Benjamin Franklin was often consulted for advice. In responding to a plea for guidance from fellow scientist Joseph Priestly, rather than providing advice, he described how he himself made decisions—the pro/con analysis described above. Of course, there are many more analytical methods nowadays to conduct such analysis, but I have found that this method is a good starting point to help weigh the positive and negative aspects of any policy, or as Dr. Franklin called it, "prudential algebra." In some cases, this level of analysis is sufficient in the "real world" depending on how much data and academic analysis is available.

> *In the Affair of so much Importance to you, wherein you ask my Advice, I cannot for want of sufficient Premises, advise you what to determine, but if you please I will tell you how. . . . To get over this, my Way is, to divide half a Sheet of Paper by a Line into two Columns, writing over the one Pro, and over the other Con. Then during three or four Days Consideration I put down under the different Heads short Hints of the different Motives that at different Times occur to me for or against the Measure. . . . And tho' the Weight of Reasons cannot be taken with the Precision of Algebraic Quantities, yet when each is thus considered separately and comparatively, and the whole lies before me, I think I can judge better, and am less likely to take a rash Step; and in fact I have found great Advantage from this kind of Equation, in what may be called Moral or Prudential Algebra.*
>
> —Benjamin Franklin, 1772[41]

So the next step in your analysis is to conduct a pro/con analysis of the current and potential effectiveness of the status quo and your two policy options. We are going to start with effectiveness and then expand the table as we analyze the other 4Es in subsequent chapters. Here's a table you can replicate for your own analysis:

| Effectiveness | Pro | Con | Summary |
|---|---|---|---|
| Status Quo | | | |
| Option 1 | | | |
| Option 2 | | | |

For the pro/con assessment, here's where your scientific evidence becomes important. I recommend using Google Scholar to find relevant papers that provide some understanding of the effectiveness of the options and the challenges that might be faced. Google Scholar is a solid search mechanism available at no cost, and after finding one paper that way you can also look at other papers that cite it, and in that way build a solid body of evidence.

In filling out the table, you want to include a brief summary of what evidence you found supporting each pro and con and provide a citation to that work. Next, review the pro/con results and use this simple mechanism to illustrate the summary of the results. When you make this assessment, compare option 1 and option 2 to the status quo, not to each other at this stage. You want an independent assessment first. Later, you will synthesize the results together.

The system I use is:

- "+" if the pros outweigh the cons relative to the status quo.
- "–" if the cons outweigh the pros relative to the status quo.

## Step 4: Analyze the Effectiveness of the Status Quo and the Policy Options

- "0" if the pros equal the cons relative to the status quo. This should be used rarely, because including it means you really have no support for your theory of action. It typically is an indicator that you need to start analyzing a new policy option instead.

- "?" if there is insufficient data to answer the question. This should be used rarely, however, because with some work you can probably find some proximate data. Remember that policymakers still need to make a decision and some data is better than no data—even if you need to acknowledge the uncertainties.

### Food Insecurity Example

Now let's fill in the table for our food insecurity example:

- For the Status Quo, we have the output data from our preliminary research—a 60% participation rate.

- For Option 1, using Google Scholar and the search term "WIC participation," I found a paper that compared states that offered an electronic option for participating in benefits versus those that did not. Over a five-year period, the researchers found that WIC participation rates increased by a significant and sustained rate of about 8%.[42] Looking at the limitations of the study provides some cons. In particular, the program may not be effective in rural areas with limited digital resources.

- For Option 2, using the search string "WIC transportation," I found a useful paper that synthesized the results of a number of papers. That paper identified a number of studies indicating that although transportation was an contributive factor in WIC participation for most, transportation was primarily important for specific populations, including pregnant teenagers and Spanish speakers.[43]

We can thus bring these results into the table seen here.

| Effectiveness | Pro | Con | Summary |
|---|---|---|---|
| Status Quo: USDA WIC Program | WIC is a cost-effective program in providing nutritious diets that improve children's health and academic achievement. | Only 60% of families eligible for WIC participate. | - |
| Option 1: Digital application and benefits | Study found that use of digital benefits increased participation by 8%.[39] | Digital benefits may not work as well in rural areas with limited access.[39] | + |
| Option 2: Transportation voucher | Study found that when transportation is a significant barrier it impacts 4–10% of the population.[40] | Transportation issues were cited by a limited population, primarily pregnant teenagers and Spanish speakers.[40] | + |

### Tip: Look for Effectiveness Analysis in Gray Literature

As discussed earlier, effectiveness is the key "E" where existing scientific literature can play a role in your policy analysis. For many scientists and engineers, however, this is the point where their work will need to interface with studies in the social sciences to better understand the relationship of their idea with human behavior. In addition, relevant work may be in the "gray literature"—research work conducted by government agencies and national laboratories that may or may not go through an external peer review process. Fortunately, today, more and more academic researchers are participating in centers that bring together the life sciences, physical sciences, engineering, and the social sciences with a focus on specific societal challenges like health, energy, and the environment. This enhances the data available for policy analysis and policymaking.

## Step 4: Analyze the Effectiveness of the Status Quo and the Policy Options

### Thought Exercise 5: Develop Your Pro/Con Analysis of the Effectiveness of the Status Quo and Two Policy Options

Fill out the pro/con effectiveness table below for the status quo and your policy options.

Note that the goal here is primarily a learning exercise. Once you have found at least one research paper to support your analysis you can stop, because you have sufficient information to move to the next step. A true analysis will take much longer. For now, I just want you to learn the steps in the policy analysis process. If interested, you can always go back and expand later.

| Effectiveness | Pro | Con | Summary |
|---|---|---|---|
| Status Quo | | | |
| Option 1 | | | |
| Option 2 | | | |

# Chapter 6
## Step 5: Analyze the Efficiency of the Status Quo and the Policy Options

Though my first high school foray into scientific research didn't have the societal impact I was hoping for, I remained as committed as ever to using my scientific and technical talents to solve societal problems. I was in my late 20s, in the midst of my PhD program learning about how to conduct policy analysis at American University in Washington, DC, when I joined the staff of the National Academies of Sciences, Engineering, and Medicine (NASEM). There, I worked as a program officer writing science and technology policy reports based on the consensus of volunteers who brought their scientific and technical knowledge to bear on societal challenges.

My first study, requested by Congress, was on the policy implications of greenhouse warming (what today we would call climate change). It was the early 1990s; the expert committee was chaired by a former senator and governor from the state of Washington who held an engineering degree and included about 50 prominent individuals, including some future Nobel prize winners and future heads of major federal research agencies. As an engineer, I was in charge of the mitigation portion of the study, assessing all the various ways for the U.S. to reduce greenhouse gas emissions: carbon dioxide ($CO_2$), methane, and the like.

Most of my work was identifying what mitigation methods would be the most effective in reducing greenhouse gas emissions. For example, switching to renewable sources of electricity could have a huge impact on reducing $CO_2$, because many of the services we need as a society today (and in the future) rely on electricity.

By that time I had spent five years as a field engineer implementing air pollution policy and as a volunteer focused on Texas state politics, so I better understood the challenges faced in getting action on renewable energy and other mitigation methods. I was optimistic, however, about making a difference because the study had been requested by Congress, so at least some policymakers were interested in hearing what scientific and technical experts had to say. Yet I still had so much to learn beyond my academic training. In particular, an analysis of effectiveness was not enough to move the needle on policy actions.

## Step 5: Analyze the Efficiency of the Status Quo and the Policy Options

A dinner one night with some of the committee experts was the first step to me gaining a "policy mindset" instead of just a "scientific and engineering effectiveness mindset." During the dinner, William Nordhaus, an economist who later went on to win the Nobel Prize, asked a series of questions to the 20 or so experts (and me!) who were sitting around the dinner table. Try to answer these questions as you read them:

- What are all the societal problems we have in the world?
- What is your income?
- If you knew climate change was definitely going to occur, what percentage of your income would you voluntarily contribute to combat climate change?

The answer to that last question ranged from 0.01% to 10%. I have since asked this question innumerable times when I've sat with other experts, as well as students young and old, and I've always gotten this same range.

Why the difference? One reason may be how much disposable income each of us have. As a graduate student living in an expensive city, I had practically none, so my answer was one of the lowest. Others might consider it more important to spend their disposable income on homelessness, lack of clean drinking water, disease, and hunger—all of which climate change will likely exacerbate, but even if climate change were somehow fully solved, these would still be fundamental long-term problems. Some people actually resent the focus on climate change in light of these other societal ills.

At this point, I began to recognize that if I wanted to impact policymaking, I needed to know more than just how effective a scientific and technical option was. Instead, I needed to think like a policymaker. I needed to include other factors in my assessment—like how much an action would cost relative to its impact, who would be adversely affected, and who was likely to support or oppose the action.

If you want to make an impact with your scientific and technical expertise, you'll need to do the same. You'll need to go beyond effectiveness as policymakers, and the public needs more than that information to make an evidence-based decision. Yet providing efficiency data that incorporates cost is not common in S&T policy studies. Out of the about 50 studies I staffed during my 18 years at the National Academies, only two looked at the costs of the policies that were being recommended. Those two, both congressionally requested studies, were the ones I described earlier on climate change and U.S. competitiveness, and I believe had the most impact of all the studies I worked on while at the NASEM.

## What Is Benefit-Cost Analysis?

Benefit-cost analysis (BCA) analyzes the societal benefits and costs of a policy, program, project, regulation, or other government action to all members of society. It is also called cost-benefit analysis, but since the calculation (shown below) involves subtracting costs from benefits, most analysts prefer the use of the former rather than the latter.

*Net Benefit = Incremental Benefits - Incremental Costs*

In the United States, Executive Order 12291 requires executive agencies to perform benefit-cost analysis as well as regulatory impact analysis for all major rules.[44] This executive order, which has been in place since 1981, was first signed by President Ronald Reagan, and each president since then has supported the rule. In addition, many states require benefit-cost analysis for their policies, including those related to economic development, health and social services, environment, education, and transportation.

The biggest challenge in BCA is determining the incremental societal benefits—that is, the increase in benefits relative to the status quo. In health policy, some prefer to use variations such as cost-effectiveness analysis and cost-utility analysis because they do not require quantifying the benefits of a human life or the quality with which that life is lived. We are going to focus only on BCA in this chapter, but there are many resources available to learn about the other methods, particularly from the Centers for Disease Control (CDC).

What's always important to keep in mind is that efficiency, as determined by BCA, is still only one factor in policymaking. BCA includes these 10 steps:

1. Explain the purpose of the BCA.
2. Specify the set of alternative projects.
3. Decide whose benefits and costs count (specify standing).
4. Identify the impact categories, catalogue them, and select metrics.
5. Predict the impacts quantitatively over the life of the project.
6. Monetize (attach dollar values) to all impacts.
7. Discount benefits and costs to obtain present values.[45]
8. Compute the net present value of each alternative.
9. Perform sensitivity analysis.
10. Make a recommendation.[46]

# Step 5: Analyze the Efficiency of the Status Quo and the Policy Options

## Find Benefit-Cost Analysis

Here's the good news. In general, you are not conducting this analysis yourself but rather relying on the work of others who are BCA specialists. I present the steps above, however, as it is important as a policy analyst to understand the difference between a good and a bad BCA.

Conducting a BCA requires a great deal of judgment, so it is easy to succumb to bias based on what benefits and costs are included and the degree to which you conduct sensitivity analysis (basically assessing the uncertainty of the analysis by changing key variables). So, in a classroom setting when I'm teaching BCA, I have students review a real-world analysis by looking to see if each of the above steps is followed. They almost uniformly find a nuance with which they disagree or else realize that a sensitivity analysis has not been conducted. You should do the same in identifying appropriate benefit-cost analysis to analyze the efficiency of your policy options.

So how do you undertake your own analysis? Here's a simple approach:

- Identify each option's three most important costs.
- Identify each option's three most important benefits.
- Go to Google Scholar to see if there is a benefit-cost analysis you can use for those costs. They might not be for your specific situation, but you can use them to develop a reasonable estimate.
- If you are unable to find a BCA for your benefits and costs, then you will need to develop a "back of the envelope" calculation instead based on whatever data you can find.

## Develop a Pro/Con Efficiency Analysis of Status Quo and Policy Options

Once you figure out your benefits and costs, you need to record the results in a table like the one you developed for effectiveness, so we can begin to bring together the data for all 4Es at the end.

| Efficiency | Pro | Con | Summary |
|---|---|---|---|
| Status Quo | | | |
| Option 1 | | | |
| Option 2 | | | |

## Food Insecurity Example

Here's our food insecurity example to illustrate how to estimate the benefits and costs.

- For the status quo, I used Google Scholar to find relevant papers on benefit-cost analysis for the WIC program using the search string "benefit-cost analysis wic program." This brought up a number of useful articles. I then went to the WIC website to find how much the WIC program cost per person today. Using this information, I could calculate the total costs. For non-monetary considerations, I was able to find useful information on the WIC program website.

- For Option 1, I used Google Scholar with the search string "online application WIC program" and found a number of interesting articles. One discussed the effectiveness of telehealth programs with program participants and recommended further use of such programs.

- For Option 2, I tried Google Scholar but was unable to find a useful article on travel vouchers except for one article that said there was insufficient information. I then went to the main Google search engine and found information from a program focused on helping those in rural communities, which described how programs worked but had no information on cost. So I resorted to finding the average cost of a ride with national rideshare companies to develop an estimate.

## Step 5: Analyze the Efficiency of the Status Quo and the Policy Options

Here are the results for the status quo:

| WIC Program Budget: $6 billion 2023 | | |
|---|---|---|
| **Benefits (measurement method)** | **Costs (measurement method)** | **Nonmonetary Considerations[47]** |
| Prenatal WIC enrollment reduced first year medical costs for U.S. infants by $1.19 billion in 1992.[48] | WIC recipients increase (Average monthly food costs per person $48 in 2021.[49]) | Improves cognitive development (vocabulary scores and memory) |
| For each $1.00 spent on WIC services, Medicaid savings in costs for newborn medical care were $2.91.[50] | | Improved likelihood of regular medical care and up to date immunizations |
| WIC benefits pay for itself within one year. For each federal dollar spent, between $2.89 and $3.50 was saved during the first 18 years.[51] | | Reduces fetal deaths and infant mortality |

Now let's determine the costs for Option 1 and Option 2. These costs include both the direct costs for implementing each measure and also an increase in the benefits paid by the program as more women participate.

**Direct Program Costs:**
1. For Option 1, the direct costs are minimal for website development and staffing for digital applications and benefits.[52]

2. For Option 2, the direct costs for the transportation vouchers are about $25 per visit,[53] with about four visits per year.

**Cost to Support Increase in Program Participation:**
3. For both Option 1 and Option 2, based on our effectiveness analysis, we can expect about 8% increase in WIC program participation. The data for Option 1 had greater certainty than for Option 2 based on the papers

presented. It does seem, however, that there is not a substantial difference in participation rates between the two options.

4. Approximately 1.4 million women participated in the program on behalf of themselves and their children in 2021.[54] So we can use this number for the costs, but the number with the children who benefit is much higher—around 6.2 million.

5. If we multiply the percent increase (0.08) times the number of women (1.4 million), that means a 0.1 million increase in participation rates.

**Results:**
6. For Option 1, the program implementation costs are minimal and part of existing funding. There will, however, be an increase in benefits provided: (0.1 million women)($48/person funding) = $4.8 million. This is probably a low estimate because the available data is per person and the family may or may not include additional people (infants and children). But it is a reasonable estimate for now.

7. For Option 2, the program implementation costs are (0.1 million women) ($25 voucher/visit)(4 visits/year) = $10 million/year for this program. There are administrative costs as well related to reimbursement and the like, based on how current programs work, but we're going to assume that, as with Option 1, this can be incorporated into the existing budget. We're also going to assume that the cost for the additional food provided to families is the same as in Option 1—about $4.8 million.

8. In Sum:
    a. Option 1 Annual Cost Estimate: $4.8 million
    b. Option 2 Annual Cost Estimate: $4.8 million + $10 million = $14.8 million
    c. The WIC budget is $5.0 billion ($5000 million), so we're looking at a budget increase of 0.1% for Option 1 and 0.3% for Option 2. In both cases, this seems to be a reasonable investment relative to the overall budget.

For benefits, we have a number of estimates in the status quo table above, but the one that seems most relevant is $2.91 benefit in Medicare cost savings per $1 WIC program investment (the average of the numbers in the first column, last row, of the status quo cost table). In this case, it makes the most sense to focus on the increased food investment as opposed to the program cost. Based on our calculation in number 8 above for both options, that is $4.8 million. So our calculation is:

## Step 5: Analyze the Efficiency of the Status Quo and the Policy Options

($2.91 benefit in Medicare cost savings/WIC program investment)($4.8 million increase in WIC program food investment) = $14 million.

|  | Benefit | Cost |
|---|---|---|
| **Option 1: Digital application and benefits** | $14 million | $4.8 Million |
| **Option 2: Transportation voucher** | $14 million | $14.8 million |

So this would imply that it would make sense to move forward with Option 1, because the societal benefits are greater than societal costs. For Option 2, however, the costs are slightly higher than the benefits. When we incorporate the nonmonetary considerations, however, it still seems reasonable to move forward with Option 2 given the small difference between the benefits and the costs.

We now bring these results into the table seen here.

| Efficiency | Pro | Con | Summary |
|---|---|---|---|
| **Status Quo: USDA WIC Program** | The federal government receives a financial benefit for every dollar invested in the WIC program. For each $1.00 spent on WIC services, Medicaid savings in costs for newborn medical care were $2.91. | A large number of eligible women do not participate in the program, resulting in increased Medicaid costs. | - |
| **Option 1: Digital application and benefits** | The benefits of implementing this program exceed the costs. | The technical nature of the staff needed for this program may result in higher staff program costs. | ++ |
| **Option 2: Transportation voucher** | The benefits of implementing this program are about the same as the costs. | Staff time will be needed to identify transportation partners willing to participate in the program. | + |

This is a reasonable back-of-the-envelope estimate, supported by scientific papers and timely data. If I were doing this analysis for a real-life policymaker, however, I would consult with a number of people. Most important would be those involved in the WIC program administration of the states that have initiated either online registration or transportation aid, the interest groups advocating for these actions, and the researchers from whom I gathered the cost estimates. I would have them look at this analysis (and the entire 4E analysis) to obtain their feedback. Undoubtedly, adjustments would be made. However, it's always good to have a starting point for discussion.

Another challenge in this benefit-cost analysis is that the federal agency that received the benefits (Medicaid) is not the same agency paying for the costs (WIC). What's more, WIC program funding is distributed to the states so if they invest in these programs, they won't accrue the benefit unless there is some redistribution of funds or financial incentives provided by the federal government. This may be part of the reason some of these actions have not already been implemented. This is a topic that might be worthy of policymaker discussion.

> **Tip: Ballpark Benefit-Cost Analysis Is Better than No Analysis**

I hope you see the usefulness of putting together even a ballpark benefit-cost analysis for policymakers. Policymakers do understand overall agency budgets, because all of them are involved in the annual budgeting process. However, when it comes to the nuances of implementing a specific program, they likely have no idea. So one question you may be asked when meeting with a policymaker to pitch your idea is "So, how much will this cost?" You need to have an answer ready. When you take the time to compute the costs, they may well be reasonable and actually enhance your proposal's desirability.

## Step 5: Analyze the Efficiency of the Status Quo and the Policy Options

### Thought Exercise 6: Develop Your Pro/Con Analysis of the Efficiency of the Status Quo and Two Policy Options

Develop the content for the pro/con efficiency table in this chapter for the status quo and your policy options. As noted with the effectiveness exercise, this is just a learning exercise. Try to find a benefit-cost analysis for your status quo and options and, if not, develop a ballpark estimate.

Even a simple low-medium-high helps think through what you ultimately want to know—which option will get the best bang for the buck. As long as your thought process is clear, it is sufficient for this exercise.

| Efficiency | Pro | Con | Summary |
|---|---|---|---|
| Status Quo | | | |
| Option 1 | | | |
| Option 2 | | | |

# Chapter 7

## Step 6: Analyze the Equity of the Status Quo and the Policy Options

We all want a world that is fair to everyone. Reaching that equity goal is challenging and can take decades or even centuries. An equity policy issue I learned about in my consulting work in West Virginia—one of the poorest states in the country—is the challenges related to flooding. Personally, I had no idea of these inequities and just assumed that any time a flooding event occurred, help was on the way from the federal government. Here, for example, is a 2021 National Public Radio story that visited the town of Rainelle, West Virginia, after a major flood impacted the state in 2016:

> Rainelle is one of hundreds of small towns where climate driven flooding potentially poses an existential threat. . . . When large numbers of people don't have insurance or savings after a disaster, the effects can ripple through the community. Towns like Rainelle are a bellwether for that future. Here, flood insurance is already unaffordable for many residents, and climate-driven flood damage has already exceeded local resources. About a third of Rainelle residents live below the poverty line, and the cost of repairing the 2016 flood damage was insurmountable for many families.
>
> [Reverend] Trigg's displaced congregants would call him, hopeless, in the months after the flood. "A lot of people in Rainelle were poor, and they didn't have any insurance. They didn't have any way to have any backup plan," he says.
>
> With no money for repairs, many people took what they could salvage and left Rainelle for good. "It affected the spirit of the town," Trigg says. Nearly five years later, a lot of homes are gone or only partially repaired. Trigg says all but one of the families on his block left. The city government saw a 10% decrease in water utility customers, a proxy for population loss. . . . "It's shocking," says John Wyatt, a member of the Rainelle City Council.[55]

In reality, there are many challenges, and these challenges are likely to increase. Already, 90% of natural disasters in the United States are due to flooding.[56] With

## Step 6: Analyze the Equity of the Status Quo and the Policy Options

increasing extreme weather events due to climate change, these inequities are important to resolve through policy actions. Here are some examples:

- Federal Emergency Management Agency (FEMA) flood zone maps are out of date, so just because you are not in a flood zone does not mean you won't be flooded. Today, 8.7 million properties are in flood zones, but the real number is likely to be closer to 14.6 million. This means 6 million households are disadvantaged because they do not realize their homes are at risk of flooding, and so are not taking appropriate action.[57]

- Most homeowner's and renter's insurance that you buy from a commercial company does not cover flooding. Instead, you are supposed to buy flood insurance from FEMA. But even that insurance doesn't cover all your costs and is biased toward homeowners rather than renters.[58]

- These factors combine to result in even more challenges for disadvantaged populations and communities. According to the American Flood Coalition,

    > people of color, low-income people, renters, and other vulnerable populations are disproportionately affected by flood disasters due to racist and classist policies in lending, housing, and other sectors. This history of injustice has built up structural inequality—or an uneven allocation of power—to the detriment of vulnerable populations. These groups are more likely to live in a floodplain or an area that receives limited investment, and the structural inequalities only widen after a flood hits. Vulnerable populations are more likely to experience slow or incomplete recoveries and lose wealth after disasters, with Black and Hispanic households losing an average of $27,000 and $29,000 in wealth, respectively, . . .
    >
    > The federal post-disaster assistance process contributes to this phenomenon. Strict program eligibility rules leave out certain low-income applicants and some Black homeowners; policies are not always designed with renters, non-English speakers, and unbanked populations in mind; and overly complex federal assistance applications can deter low-income people and small towns from even applying.[55]

Under the Biden Administration, FEMA is making changes. Even then, it can still be challenging. For example, the cost of a flood insurance policy did not accurately reflect the true risk a home faced for flooding. It was instead based on 1% of its annual chance of flooding and its elevation. It did not include the cost of rebuilding the home. So a homeowner on the Florida coast with a high-priced home might be paying the same amount for their insurance as someone with a low-priced home in Wyoming.

The new system, called Risk Rating 2.0: Equity in Action,[59] introduced in 2021 and put in place in 2022, made the system fairer by taking into account the replacement value and a more accurate risk of flooding assessment in setting premiums. This resulted in some homeowner's and renter's flood insurance program premiums increasing and others decreasing. Some people, however, were unwilling to pay the increased premiums, leading about 425,000 to drop their insurance coverage, leaving them more vulnerable.[60] So again, we have equity challenges even with a more scientifically based policy.

In this example, we illustrate a number of equity challenges where a range of policies and programs are not necessarily fair to everyone. Individuals might

- lack the information to assess the likelihood their home will be damaged by floods relative to those in other geographic regions;

- receive fewer financial benefits because they rent instead of own their homes;

- live disproportionately in areas affected by flood disasters due to past racist and classist policies in lending and housing; and

- lose flood insurance coverage because their premiums increased beyond what they anticipated when they moved into their home.

Equity analysis is important to assess for any policy options. There are always winners and losers, and you need to understand the implications before deciding to go forward with a policy. In some cases, you may be able to modify the policy to account for some of the anticipated and unanticipated equity challenges that may arise.

## Step 6: Analyze the Equity of the Status Quo and the Policy Options

### What Is Equity?

Equity is a term that has been in policy circles for a very long-time, but the definition has not been consistent. In general, it means fairness and the importance of recognizing that there are winners and losers in any policy. Here's an academic definition: the extent to which a policy's "benefits and costs are spread among those affected in such a way that no group or individual receives less than a minimum benefit level or a maximum cost level."[61]

One of the first executive orders that President Biden issued provided a formal definition of equity that identifies specific populations of concern:

> *The term "equity" means the consistent and systematic fair, just, and impartial treatment of all individuals, including individuals who belong to underserved communities that have been denied such treatment, such as Black, Latino, and Indigenous and Native American persons, Asian Americans and Pacific Islanders and other persons of color; members of religious minorities; lesbian, gay, bisexual, transgender, and queer (LGBTQ+) persons; persons with disabilities; persons who live in rural areas; and persons otherwise adversely affected by persistent poverty or inequality.*

> *The term "underserved communities" refers to populations sharing a particular characteristic, as well as geographic communities, that have been systematically denied a full opportunity to participate in aspects of economic, social, and civic life, as exemplified by the list in the preceding definition of "equity."* [62]

I view this as a good definition, but not sufficient for all the policy challenges that face us when discussing equity, as illustrated in the example at the beginning.

Another important definition to keep in mind is the difference between "equality" and "equity." Here's the difference, described by the Annie E. Casey Foundation:

- "Equity involves trying to understand and give people what they need to enjoy full, healthy lives.

- Equality, in contrast, aims to ensure that everyone gets the same things in order to enjoy full, healthy lives. Like equity, equality aims to promote fairness and justice, but it can only work if everyone starts from the same place and needs the same things."[63]

## Develop an Equity Analysis

More than any other policy analysis method, equity analysis is an emerging field and much of it is focused only on racial equity rather than equity in general. The good news is that the methods developed for racial equity work well for other equity topics.

It's important to keep in mind that equity analysis is more than just looking at demographic data. Rather, it is best focused on the root causes of the problem. In addition, equity analysis is a case where those who are now facing, or who may face, equity issues are the experts. Listening to those individuals, rather than presuming their opinions or telling them what can help reduce their inequities, is an important skill to cultivate for a quality equity analysis.

The Annie E. Casey Foundation recommends a seven-step approach to equity analysis:

**Step 1:** Establish an understanding of equity and inclusion principles.

**Step 2:** Engage affected populations and stakeholders.

**Step 3:** Gather and analyze disaggregated data.

**Step 4:** Conduct system analysis of root causes and inequities.

**Step 5:** Identify strategies and target resources to address root causes of inequities.

**Step 6:** Conduct equity impact assessment for all policies and decision-making.

**Step 7:** Continuously evaluate effectiveness and adapt strategies.[64]

# Step 6: Analyze the Equity of the Status Quo and the Policy Options

For the purpose of this exercise, we are going to focus first on Step 6—the equity impact assessment. For this step, the foundation recommends answering the following questions as a starting point:

1. Are all racial and ethnic groups that are affected by the policy, practice, or decision at the table?

2. How will the proposed policy, practice, or decision affect each group?

3. How will the proposed policy, practice, or decision be perceived by each group?

4. Does the policy, practice, or decision worsen or ignore existing disparities?

5. Based on the above responses, what revisions are needed in the policy, practice, or decision under discussion?[65]

I've created this handy table for our policy options. I have intentionally not included question 5 because that is part of the general iterative nature of policy analysis that we will discuss at the end.

|  | Status Quo | Option 1 | Option 2 |
|---|---|---|---|
| Groups affected by policy | | | |
| Impact of policy on each group | | | |
| Perception of policy by each group | | | |
| Impact of policy on existing disparities | | | |

## Develop a Pro/Con Equity Analysis of Status Quo and Policy Options

As before, based on our equity analysis, we want to fill out this form to contribute to our synthesis analysis.

| Equity | Pro | Con | Summary |
|---|---|---|---|
| Status Quo | | | |
| Option 1 | | | |
| Option 2 | | | |

## Step 6: Analyze the Equity of the Status Quo and the Policy Options

### Food Insecurity Example

Let's fill out the table for our food insecurity example. For the status quo, some of the information is already available from our earlier analysis.

|  | Status Quo | Option 1: Digital application and benefits | Option 2: Transportation voucher |
|---|---|---|---|
| **Groups affected by policy** | Groups with the following barriers: (1) transportation and other costs to reach WIC clinics; (2) language and clinical barriers; and (3) inability to take time away from work for the application process, risking job loss and lost wages | All three groups with barriers would benefit from this option. This presumes that the website offers sufficient language options that they are no longer a barrier. | Only the first group would benefit from this option. Those with language and job challenges would not benefit as they would still have to go to the clinic in person. |
| **Impact of policy on each group** | Do not apply for WIC funding | Increased likelihood of applying for WIC benefits | Increased likelihood of applying for WIC benefits |
| **Perception of policy by each group** | Costs to participate are greater than benefits of participating in WIC program. | Benefits of participating are greater for about 8% of the population. | Benefits of participating are greater for about 8% of the population. |
| **Impact of policy on existing disparities** | This is the existing disparity. | This option helps with all disparities. | This option only helps with one disparity. |

| Equity | Pro | Con | Summary |
|---|---|---|---|
| Status Quo | WIC helps populations that participate. | About 40% of eligible participants do not participate. | − |
| Option 1: Digital application and benefits | This option helps eligible populations who face challenges related to transportation costs, language and clinical barriers, and lost employment wages. | Eligible participants without web access or a bank to accept their WIC funding will still face challenges. | ++ |
| Option 2: Transportation voucher | This option helps eligible populations who face challenges related to transportation costs. | Eligible participants will still face the challenges of language and clinical barriers and lost employment wages because in-person visits will still be required. In addition, there may be challenges for those in rural areas who may not have easily accessible transportation options compared to those in urban areas. | + |

As a reminder, our assessment above compares each option to the status quo, not to each other. Option 1, the digital option, helps on all the equity barriers identified in the scientific literature, but there are still populations that face root cause challenges such as lack of access to the internet. And this also presumes that the website developed to accept applications has options for different languages and the ability to fill out forms on a mobile device rather than a computer. So it is better but not perfect, hence the summary assessment of "++" rather than "+++." In the case of Option 2, the transportation voucher option, it does help those without transportation options but not the other equity challenges that decrease WIC participation rates.

Step 6: Analyze the Equity of the Status Quo and the Policy Options

### Tip: Equity Is More Than Demographics

No policy is perfect and each one has winners and losers. Equity is a topic where speaking "truth to power" is often challenging. Many organizations advocate equity principles, but not many take the time to identify a baseline, develop policies to enhance equity, and then measure to see if those policies work. Equity is more than improving the demographics of participation. Focusing on root causes such as where people live, transportation options, communication and financial challenges, and internet access via mobile phones are key fundamentals that need to be considered in almost every policy.

## Thought Exercise 7: Develop Your Pro/Con Analysis of the Equity of the Status Quo and Two Policy Options

Develop the content for the pro/con equity table in this chapter for the status quo and your policy options. Equity analysis is becoming increasingly common, so with luck you will find sufficient information for your analysis. Using an artificial intelligence tool, like ChatGPT or Gemini, however, can sometimes help identify logical inequities you might not have thought of.

| Equity | Pro | Con | Summary |
|---|---|---|---|
| Status Quo | | | |
| Option 1 | | | |
| Option 2 | | | |

# Chapter 8

## Step 7: Analyze the Ease of Political Acceptability of the Status Quo and the Policy Options

I really thought I was prepared for my meeting with Texas state legislators and testifying before a committee in the legislature considering container deposit legislation. This is the idea of paying a small fee (a nickel back then) when you buy a can of soda and getting the money back when you return the can, with the goal of discouraging littering and encouraging recycling.

I had written my first "policy brief" (also known as a "one-pager")—a one page, two-sided document that brought together all the evidence to support passage of the bill. I used the concept of parallel policies to include data from other states on the effectiveness of container deposit legislation. I even had a poll from the LBJ School of Public Affairs at the University of Texas at Austin that said the majority of people in Texas favored container deposit legislation.

Yet I was totally wrong about the likelihood of passage. My first recognition of the challenge ahead was when I spoke to one of the members of the committee privately in his office. I presented the key elements of my one-pager, emphasizing the effectiveness (in reducing trash), efficiency (the legislation would save money that could then be used to clean Texas highways), and equity (the importance of beautiful rural areas not being sullied by trash). The member of the Texas state legislature countered by saying he was concerned that it would decrease funding for the local boy scout troops in his district, as collecting cans was how they funded their activities.

I then visited another member of the legislature and made my policy pitch to him. Rather than being appreciative that most Texans supported the bill, he said he thought the poll respondents misunderstood what container deposit legislation was about. He said they instead thought container deposit legislation was about a policy that would make it illegal to have alcohol in the front seat of a car.

My last step was to testify before the committee. The committee meeting room was full. I was quite surprised about this, given the topic, but it was my first time in a hearing. Then the chair introduced who was in the room by welcoming the workers from a Coca-Cola company plant in Dallas that manufactured the cans. He noted that these workers, bused from Dallas to Austin for the hearing, could lose their jobs if more cans were recycled because of the passage of the legislation. Although jobs would be created in the recycling industry, workers would need to change occupations and probably employers—perhaps receiving lower pay and benefits. And, even today, soda companies are unwilling to use recycled cans for their products.[66]

At this point, I gave my testimony about the container deposit legislation and all my facts and figures, but knew it was doomed to failure. I had fallen into a common trap—I had too much faith in common sense and reasoning and too little understanding of the perspectives of the legislators and the impact of the legislation on their constituents.

## What Is Meant by Ease of Political Acceptability?

Ease of political acceptability is the degree to which not only policymakers but also key stakeholders support or oppose a current or proposed policy. In formal literature, it is called "responsiveness"—the concept that in a representative democracy, policymakers are supposed to be responsive to their constituents. Of particular interest in public policy are the stakeholders—those who are impacted by the outcome of current policy and of possible new policies.

Sometimes what is most economically efficient does not work well in terms of political acceptability. The most common example today is a carbon tax as a way of reducing greenhouse gas emissions. Economists will tell you it is the most economical way to influence behavior related to carbon emissions. We can see this when the price of gasoline increases due to market forces. During 2022, gasoline prices increased due to the Russian invasion of Ukraine and other factors.[67] A survey by the American Automobile Association (AAA) found that "64% of drivers have made significant changes to their driving habits as a response to higher gas prices this summer, with 88% of that portion reporting driving less."[68]

Around that same time, Gallup conducted a poll that found the high gas prices led Americans to rate the U.S. economy as "poor," with economic confidence the worst since the 2007–2009 recession.[69] In addition, President Biden had his lowest job approval rating of his term in the summer of 2022—in the important months leading up to the midterm elections. This was despite low unemployment rates. This quote from Brookings

# Step 7: Analyze the Ease of Political Acceptability of the Status Quo and the Policy Options

researchers I think best summarizes what "ease of political acceptability" is about and why a carbon tax won't work in the United States:

> *The administration's policy makes sense, but is difficult to explain in a sound bite. Congress is focused more on scoring points in the political game than on informing the American people. High gasoline prices anger Americans like those for no other product. Gasoline prices are apparent to all as they drive and see the price in lights along the road, and gasoline is a crucial component in many family budgets. But the American public doesn't understand who to blame in a market that is global, nuanced, and complex. And particularly in Congress, politicians aren't helping.*[70]

Another challenge with carbon taxes concerns the differing transportation options in the country. While in the Northeast and a few other locations around the country there are viable public transportation options, the same is not true in rural areas, particularly in the middle of the country. In these areas, cars are often the only form of transportation and the distances between home and work may be long. Even in parts of the Northeast where there are subway systems, such as the Washington, DC, area, the cost of housing is so high close to the city that low-income people live further out. This can create an equity issue—which is in turn an ease of political acceptability issue for policymakers who represent those parts of the country.

So ease of political acceptability is an important consideration in policymaking. It's not just opinion poll data, however. It's also a matter of who is active and passionate about the issues being discussed. We'll explore this in the next section.

## Assess the Ease of Political Acceptability of the Policy Options

When assessing ease of political acceptability, I use a process called "Prince Analysis." No, it is not named for Machiavelli's *The Prince*, but instead stands for "Probe, Interact, Calculate, and Execute." Developed by two scholars, William Coplin and Michael O'Leary, its goal was to go beyond an academic approach and apply it to practical policy analysis.[71] It applies a "theoretical framework to the politics of public policy issues, demanding that they try to identify the political consequences of a public policy and think about how the constraints resulting from those political consequences can be dealt with." Here are the steps:

**1. State the issue** as a decision that must be made sometime in the future and over which there is some disagreement in the present.

**2. Identify the actors** who influence the decision. Start with a long list, but then combine some into categories and eliminate others to a reasonable number (e.g., 5–10). Note that "actors" or "players" includes stakeholders, government officials, and politicians.

**3. Estimate the issue position, priority, and power for each actor.** These 3Ps are given a score as indicated below. Ideally, the analyst will make this assessment based on data, not just their personal impressions. For example, it may be done by looking at the position of the organization on their website, speeches made by key political actors, or quotes in news articles.

- **Position:** The degree to which the actor is for or against the proposed policy:
    - −3 means the actor is unequivocally opposed to the policy.
    - −1 or −2 means the actor is somewhat opposed.
    - 0 means the actor is neutral.
    - 1 or 2 means the actor is somewhat supportive.
    - 3 means the actor is unequivocally in favor of the policy.

- **Power:** How influential is the actor on the policy decision? Sources of power include official position, money, number of voters, and expertise.
    - 0 means the actor has no power.
    - 1 or 2 means the actor has moderate influence.
    - 3 means the actor has maximum influence.

- **Priority:** The degree to which the actor pays attention and demonstrates that the issue is important to them. It is also called salience.
    - 0 means the issue is not important to the actor.
    - 1 or 2 means it is of moderate importance to the actor.
    - 3 means it is of maximum importance to the actor.

**4. Calculate the Prince Score.**
Prince Score = Issue Position x Power x Priority (Calculation 1)
When Issue Position is 0, Power x Priority = Prince Score

## Step 7: Analyze the Ease of Political Acceptability of the Status Quo and the Policy Options

**5. Calculate the probability of support.**
- Calculation 2: Sum of all positive scores plus ½ of neutral scores
- Calculation 3: Sum of all scores; count the negative ones as though they're positive here
- Probability of Support = (Calculation 2/Calculation 3)*100
- If probability is
    - 0%, the policy will never be implemented.
    - 1–39%, the policy is unlikely to be implemented.
    - 40–59%, the policy is likely to continue being disputed.
    - 60–99%, the policy is likely to be implemented.
    - 100%, the policy is certain to be implemented, but it is not an issue.

Prince Analysis is based on educated estimates of the 3Ps so the result is not perfect, but the exercise does force you to be explicit about your political risk assumptions. It also provides insight into where you need to intervene in the political process if you want to change the outcome.

Here's an example of the process from one of my former students. She focused on an issue in her home country, South Africa.

**Step 1: State the issue.**

What actions, if any, should the South African energy agency take to respond to concerns about the source of water for hydraulic fracturing (fracking) activities in the Karoo region of South Africa?

Policy options:
- Status quo: Use freshwater, as planned in draft regulations.
- Option 1: Provide incentives to companies to use waterless fracking, a new method.
- Option 2: Mandate companies to use acid mine drainage or sewage water.

Note that there is no need to conduct a Prince Analysis for the status quo because it has already been accepted politically. So you will only need to calculate the Prince Score for options 1 and 2. Following is an illustration for Option 2.

## Step 2: Identify the actors.

- South African government
- Shale gas companies
- Academic organizations
- Environmental organizations
- Public

## Step 3: Estimate the issue position, priority, and power for each actor.

| Actor | Position | Power | Priority |
|---|---|---|---|
| South African government | 3 | 3 | 2 |
| Shale gas companies | −3 | 2 | 2 |
| Academic organizations | 0 | 1 | 1 |
| Environmental organizations | 2 | 2 | 3 |
| Public | 2 | 1 | 3 |

Step 7: Analyze the Ease of Political Acceptability
of the Status Quo and the Policy Options

**Step 4: Calculate the Prince Score.**
Prince Score = Issue position x Power x Priority (Calculation 1)
When Issue Position is 0, Power x Priority=Prince Score. This is called a neutral score. You can see an example below for academic organizations.

| Actor | Position | Power | Priority | Prince Score |
|---|---|---|---|---|
| South African government | 3 | 3 | 2 | 18 |
| Shale gas companies | −3 | 2 | 2 | −12 |
| Academic organizations | 0 | 1 | 1 | 1 |
| Environmental organizations | 2 | 2 | 3 | 12 |
| Public | 2 | 1 | 3 | 6 |

**Step 5 Calculate the probability of support.**

Calculation 2 = Sum of the positive scores + ½ neutral scores = 18 + 12 + 6 + ½ (1) = 36.5
Calculation 3 = Sum of all scores ignoring signs = 18 + 12 + 1 + 12 + 6 = 49
Probability = Calculation 2/Calculation 3 = (36.5/49)*100 = 75%

**Result: A South African policy that would mandate companies use acid mine drainage or sewage water for hydraulic fracturing is likely to be implemented.**

From Expertise to Impact

## Develop a Pro/Con Ease of Acceptability Analysis of the Status Quo and Two Options

As before, based on our ease of political acceptability analysis, we want to fill out the form below to contribute to our synthesis analysis. One item to note is that ease of political acceptability for the status quo will almost always be positive unless there are riots in the streets (which does happen, but rarely). This is because the status quo policy has already gained political acceptability, which makes it difficult to change.

| Ease of Political Acceptability | Pro | Con | Summary |
|---|---|---|---|
| Status Quo | | | |
| Option 1 | | | |
| Option 2 | | | |

## Food Insecurity Example

Here's the summary Prince Analysis table for option 1 and option 2. As a reminder, our question is:

> *What actions, if any, should the administrator at the U.S. Department of Agriculture Food and Nutrition Service (FNS) take to respond to equity concerns about federal nutrition assistance programs, particularly for households with children headed by a single woman that have the highest rate of food insecurity in the United States?*

## Step 7: Analyze the Ease of Political Acceptability of the Status Quo and the Policy Options

The difference in the analysis of the options below is primarily due to the degree to which states have incorporated these methods into their current processes. While several states have already adopted digital applications and benefits, the same is not true of the transportation voucher option. Policymakers are more likely to prefer a known policy where they have a good understanding of the other 4Es than one where the method of implementation is less known.

**Option 1: Digital application and benefits**

| Actor | Position | Power | Priority | Prince Score |
|---|---|---|---|---|
| USDA/FNS | 2 | 3 | 2 | 12 |
| Policymakers concerned about "welfare moms" taking advantage of the system[72] | -3 | 3 | 2 | -18 |
| Food advocacy organizations | 3 | 1 | 3 | 9 |
| Academic experts | 0 | 1 | 1 | 1 |
| Food insecure women with children | 3 | 1 | 3 | 9 |

Calculation 2 = Sum of the positive scores + ½ neutral scores = 12 + 9 + 9 + ½ (1) = 30.5
Calculation 3 = Sum of all scores ignoring signs = 12 + 18 + 9 + 1 + 9 = 49
Probability = Calculation 2/Calculation 3 = (30.5/49)*100 = 62%

## Option 2: Transportation voucher

| Actor | Position | Power | Priority | Prince Score |
|---|---|---|---|---|
| USDA/FNS | 1 | 3 | 1 | 3 |
| Policymakers concerned about "welfare moms" taking advantage of the system | –3 | 3 | 2 | -18 |
| Food advocacy organizations | +3 | 2 | 1 | 6 |
| Academic experts | 0 | 1 | 1 | 1 |
| Food insecure women with children | 3 | 1 | 3 | 9 |

Calculation 2 = Sum of the positive scores + ½ neutral scores = 3+6+9+ ½ (1) = 18.5
Calculation 3 = Sum of all scores ignoring signs = 3+18+6+1+9 = 37
Probability = Calculation 2/Calculation 3 =(18.5/37)*100=50%

## Step 7: Analyze the Ease of Political Acceptability of the Status Quo and the Policy Options

The probability calculation provides guidance for assessing the ease of acceptability for each policy as illustrated below.

| Ease of Political Acceptability | Pro | Con | Summary |
|---|---|---|---|
| Status Quo | States have the ability to provide digital options and transportation vouchers if they wish. | About 40% of eligible participants do not participate in the WIC program due to challenges. Some conservative states are unlikely to consider options to encourage participation. | ++ |
| Option 1: Digital application and benefits | Some states are already implementing this option. (Prince probability of action: 62%) | Some state policymakers will oppose making it easier to get WIC benefits. | + |
| Option 2: Transportation voucher | No states are implementing this option thus far for this purpose. (Prince probability of action: 50%) | Some state policymakers will oppose making it easier to get WIC benefits. | − |

### Tip: Not Everyone Will Love Your Policy Options

The ease of political acceptability is an important assessment to understand the key players and their position for any policy. There are always policymakers and interest groups who will oppose any policy.

Sometimes students tell me that no one opposes their policy. Then I ask, "If it's such a good idea, why isn't it already being implemented?" There is a reason, and you just need to find why people either oppose it or don't make it a high enough priority so it gets funding.

If you look for the opposition, it's there, and you need to account for it in your analysis. If you're an advocacy organization, it's also a good way to see if you can win moderate organizations to your side by tweaking your policy option so they are willing to support it. And when you meet with a policymaker, they're sure to ask you who opposes your proposed policy and why. You need to be ready to answer that question.

## Step 7: Analyze the Ease of Political Acceptability of the Status Quo and the Policy Options

### Thought Exercise 8: Develop Your Pro/Con Analysis of the Ease of Political Acceptability of the Status Quo and Two Policy Options

Develop the content for the pro/con ease of political acceptability table in this chapter for the status quo and your policy options.

One way to find those who disagree with a policy option is to use search terms like "oppose WIC program." Suddenly you'll find articles from organizations that oppose the policy, don't believe the scientific evidence, or have general principles that oppose the policy. Tools like ChatGPT and Bard can also help you understand why there is opposition to a policy option as they gather information from across the internet.

Another good way to find who opposes a policy is to ask those who support it. They'll easily be able to answer the question as they often participate in the same events, testify at hearings, or write articles opposing the other's viewpoints in opinion sections of media organizations.

| Ease of Political Acceptability | Pro | Con | Summary |
|---|---|---|---|
| Status Quo | | | |
| Option 1 | | | |
| Option 2 | | | |

Congratulations! You have finished your 4E analysis and are ready to put together all the pieces of your analysis!

# Chapter 9

# Step 8: Synthesize the Results of the 4E Analysis

When I was working on the *Rising Above the Gathering Storm* study, I prepared congressional testimony for several members of the committee that developed the report. One time it was for the chair of the committee, Norman Augustine—a former CEO of Lockheed Martin and Department of Defense official, an engineer, and a Republican. He is one of the most skilled individuals I know in science and technology policy communication.

When I prepared the draft of his testimony—which was five pages because statements are typically limited to five minutes—I spent one page on why taking action on U.S. competitiveness was important and four pages outlining our four recommendations. I thought this was a good design that covered the essentials of the material. But when Mr. Augustine reviewed the material, he asked me to rewrite the testimony doing the reverse—four pages to focus on why U.S. competitiveness was a problem for the nation, and one page on our policy recommendations. I asked him why, and he told me that we must first convince the policymakers there is a big problem before we can get them to listen to our solutions.

Once I rewrote the testimony, I could see what he meant. In addition, when describing the problem, he would sprinkle in all sorts of mini-anecdotes that illustrated what he was talking about. If you look at the beginning of the *Gathering Storm* report, you'll see several pages of these anecdotes that he would draw upon not only in testimony but when meeting individually with members of the Cabinet and members of Congress.

He was explaining the issue through stories that everyone could understand. As Albert Einstein once said, "You do not really understand something unless you can explain it to your grandmother" (attributed). To be good science and technology policy communicators, we'll need our facts and figures, but we'll also need the anecdotes that personalize the story so policymakers can see who they are helping if they take action on your proposed policy.

## Step 8: Synthesize the Results of the 4E Analysis

### Develop a Pro/Con Table Bringing Together Your 4E Analysis

In this step, you'll bring together the results of the pro/con tables you put together for each of the 4Es. Keep in mind that until this stage, you were independently comparing Option 1 and Option 2 relative to the status quo. In this table, you now compare all three together in the table here.

|  | Effectiveness | Efficiency | Equity | Ease of Political Acceptability |
|---|---|---|---|---|
| Status Quo |  |  |  |  |
| Option 1 |  |  |  |  |
| Option 2 |  |  |  |  |

Now is a good time to ask yourself questions such as these before solidifying your decision:

- If your idea is such a good one, why is it not being implemented already? Should this aspect be incorporated into your analysis?

- Is your projection realistic? Or are you letting your personal bias sway you?

- What if the key variable(s) in your design was the opposite of what you projected? This sensitivity analysis helps you identify the uncertainty in your analysis.

- In the end, how confident are you in your analysis?

After answering these questions, adjust your analysis if necessary, and then you are ready to go to the next step.

## From Expertise to Impact

## Food Insecurity Example

For our food insecurity example, we bring together our pluses and minuses from all the previous tables as shown here.

|  | Effectiveness | Efficiency | Equity | Ease of Political Acceptability |
|---|---|---|---|---|
| Status Quo: USDA WIC Program | − | − | − | ++ |
| Option 1: Digital application and benefits | + | ++ | ++ | + |
| Option 2: Transportation voucher | + | + | + | − |

You should be able to glance at this table and clearly see why each assessment is the way it is based not on opinion but on evidence as built through the previous chapters. In this case, for example, you should be able to clearly explain why the ease of political acceptability assessment differs for each option.

Note that we don't present this behind-the-scenes work to policymakers. Rather, it provides a way for us to internally think through our assessment of each of the 4Es for each option, so it is clear how we make the final recommendation in the next step.

## Tip: Yes, You Can Adjust Your Analysis

Remember, it's not too late to make adjustments if you lack confidence. That's why it's good to ask colleagues what they think. Policy analysis is a constantly iterative process.

## Step 8: Synthesize the Results of the 4E Analysis

You learn and understand more, and sometimes you need to go back to the beginning or to your analysis of one of the 4Es. You're learning, not failing. Better to have confidence that you have done the best analysis you can with the available data and resources you have than to face a policymaker later who asks why you didn't take action when you had the chance.

From Expertise to Impact

## Thought Exercise 9: Bring Your 4E Analysis Together

Bring your 4E pro/con analysis together for the status quo and your policy options in your final table. Be sure to review your analysis with others and answer the following questions with others:

- If your idea is such a good one, why is it not being implemented already? Should this aspect be incorporated into your analysis?

- Is your projection realistic, or are you letting your personal bias sway you?

- What if the key variable(s) in your design was the opposite of what you projected? This sensitivity analysis helps you identify the uncertainty in your analysis.

- In the end, how confident are you in your analysis?

|  | Effectiveness | Efficiency | Equity | Ease of Political Acceptability |
|---|---|---|---|---|
| Status Quo |  |  |  |  |
| Option 1 |  |  |  |  |
| Option 2 |  |  |  |  |

# Chapter 10
## Step 9: Decide What Policy Option(s) to Present or Recommend

One conversation with Senator Lamar Alexander really stuck with me throughout the years. Senator Alexander, a Republican from Tennessee, was one of the strongest supporters of funding for research and STEM education. He came from a state that had a strong scientific and technical workforce in Oak Ridge National Laboratory. He'd previously served as president of the University of Tennessee, governor of Tennessee, and U.S. Secretary of Education in the George H.W. Bush administration. So he was someone who really knew the scientific and technical community and had an honest relationship with its members.

Senator Alexander told me and others in a meeting that many scientists and engineers would come to him with ideas, but he had no way of knowing which ones were better. He was willing to advocate among his fellow senators for those ideas, but he needed the right knowledge himself in order to be successful. What he needed was for these ideas to be ranked in order of priority. His previous interactions had not provided him with that information. This led to the following questions being addressed in the study:

- What are the top 10 actions, in priority order, that federal policymakers could take to enhance the science and technology enterprise so that the United States can successfully compete, prosper, and be secure in the global community of the 21st century?

- What implementation strategy, with several concrete steps, could be used to implement each of those actions?[73]

The committee that wrote the report ended up with four recommendations and a back-of-the-envelope cost estimate for each one of those actions. Those four recommendations, in priority order, were:

1. **10,000 Teachers, 10 Million Minds:** Increase the U.S. talent pool by vastly improving K–12 science and mathematics education.

2. **Sowing the Seeds:** Sustain and strengthen the nation's traditional commitment to long-term basic research that has the potential to be transformational. This should maintain the flow of new ideas that fuel the economy, provide security, and enhance the quality of life.

3. **Best and Brightest:** Make the U.S. the most attractive setting in which to study and perform research so that we can develop, recruit, and retain the best and brightest students, scientists, and engineers from within the U.S. and throughout the world.

4. **Incentives for Innovation:** Ensure that the U.S. is the premier place in the world to innovate. This will take the form of investing in downstream activities, such as manufacturing and marketing, and creating high-paying jobs based on innovation by modernizing the patent system, realigning tax policies to encourage innovation, and ensuring affordable broadband access.

Although these actions were prioritized, the committee also emphasized the importance of taking action in the four recommendations, recognizing the importance of the scientific and technical enterprise as a system rather than a series of piecemeal fields. They stated:

> The committee members deeply believe in the fundamental linkage of all the recommendations and their integrity as a coordinated set of policy actions. To emphasize one or neglect another, the members decided, would substantially weaken what should be viewed as a coherent set of high-priority actions to create jobs and enhance the nation's energy supply in an era of globalization. For example, there is little benefit in producing more researchers if there are no funds to support their research.[74]

There were, of course, many bills in Congress that supported each of these recommendations, but I believe the key to the success of the initiative that resulted in the America COMPETES Act not just initially but in subsequent updates of the Act was taking this systems approach and providing estimated costs for each of the proposed actions.

## Step 9: Decide What Policy Option(s) to Present or Recommend

> **Decide!**

By putting your analysis together in step 8, you should be able to easily see which option makes the most sense to recommend. In checking your decision, it's always good to talk to colleagues to get their thoughts on your analysis and final decision. Here's a list of questions to ask yourself:

- Imagine you are the policymaker to whom you are addressing your analysis. What questions do you think they would ask you about your recommendation?

- Imagine then that the policymaker asks you to implement your recommendation. What would you want to know? Have you thought through the implementation steps? For example, how might the policy be enforced?

- If you have a hard time deciding among your options, you may need to go back and look at your analysis.

    - Have you differentiated the options from each other enough?

    - Do you need to reconceptualize your policymaker, question, policy options, analysis, tradeoffs, and/or costs?

    - If you want to recommend both options, then you need to bring those two options together in a single option and then identify another alternative option to analyze.

- Finally, try explaining your analysis and final decision to a friend and ask them to be a devil's advocate. If you feel confident after that discussion, your decision is ready!

Now you just need to summarize it in a paragraph, using the 4Es to say why you are recommending this policy option.

A final note, however, is that in some situations, you don't want to decide and instead just present options. For example, at the Congressional Research Service, where I worked, you were not allowed to make recommendations. This is fine, but you should still be able to briefly describe the pros and cons of each action so your policymaker can easily decide.

## Food Insecurity Example

In our food security example, you should be able to clearly see that Option 1, the digital application and benefits options, makes the most sense based on the 4Es.

|  | Effectiveness | Efficiency | Equity | Ease of Political Acceptability |
|---|---|---|---|---|
| Status Quo: USDA WIC Program | - | - | - | ++ |
| Option 1: Digital application and benefits | + | ++ | ++ | + |
| Option 2: Transportation voucher | + | + | + | - |

So in the end, how do we answer our original question:

> *What actions, if any, should the administrator at the U.S. Department of Agriculture Food and Nutrition Service (FNS) take to respond to equity concerns about federal nutrition assistance programs, particularly for households with children headed by a single woman that have the highest rate of food insecurity in the United States?*

Here are the key points in Option 1 for each of the 4Es from the pro side in our 4E tables.

- **Effectiveness:** Study found that use of digital benefits increased participation by 8%.

- **Efficiency:** For each $1.00 spent on WIC services, Medicaid savings in costs for newborn medical care were $2.91. The benefits exceed the costs.

## Step 9: Decide What Policy Option(s) to Present or Recommend

- **Equity:** Three groups with barriers to applying for WIC and receiving funds are those who have (1) transportation and other costs to reach WIC clinics; (2) language and clinical barriers; and (3) jobs where applying for services requires time away from work, risking job loss and lost wages. All three of these groups with barriers would benefit from a digital registration option.

- **Ease of Political Acceptability:** Some states are already implementing this option.

We can now compare the 4Es for each option to make the evidence behind the decision clear:

*The USDA FNS administrator should take steps to require that states provide a digital option for eligible women to apply for the WIC program and receive their benefits. Taking this step is likely to increase the effectiveness of the program in reaching those who currently do not participate by approximately 8% relative to the status quo.*

*The implementation costs for this option are lower than the alternative of providing a transportation voucher, which would also likely require additional staff support. Once benefits are received, research indicates that newborns receiving WIC benefits are less likely to need as much funding from Medicaid.*

*This recommendation will also help the USDA provide more equitable access to WIC benefits by reducing the need for transportation for those without vehicles, minimizing time away from work for those employed, and centralizing support to non-English-speaking clients by easily providing multiple language options.*

*Several states have already implemented the digital option voluntarily, showing that it is possible to provide this service with current resources alleviating the need for additional financial and, thus, political support. Since the transportation voucher option has not been implemented and is more expensive than the digital option, it is less likely that it will be supported by states or policymakers.*

## Tip: The Status Quo May Be the Best Option

Realistically, the status quo—no additional action—is the most likely action. Change is difficult and policymakers will need to decide if the likelihood of success is worth the effort. In our food insecurity example, the data indicate that implementing either alternative will increase participation by 8%. For some policymakers, 8% will be too low. For others, it is sufficient. This decision will often depend on their constituents. For example, policymakers representing urban areas with public transportation options and populations where almost everyone speaks English may not think the proposed options sufficiently help their constituents. So don't be afraid to say that no additional action is necessary at this time. It may well be the right decision for the policymaker for whom you are preparing your analysis.

## Step 9: Decide What Policy Option(s) to Present or Recommend

### Thought Exercise 10: Make Your Recommendation

Write a paragraph making your recommendation clear based on your 4E analysis. Begin by putting together four bullets that highlight why you think your preferred option is the best option when comparing the 4Es. Note that this does not mean that your option is the clear winner for each "E." In our food insecurity analysis, for example, the effectiveness of both options is about the same. You just need to be clear why your option is better than the status quo, or alternatively why sticking with the status quo makes the most sense.

# Chapter 11

# Step 10: Communicate the Results of Your Analysis

Although we have spoken a great deal about evidence-based analysis and data, it's important not to lose sight of the fact that anecdotal evidence conveys the emotion behind the societal impact, which is also important.

A good example is the State of the Union Address, the annual speech each U.S. president gives to a joint session of Congress about how the country is doing, which provides the key elements of that year's budget request. During the speech, presidents typically recognize people whom they have invited to be part of the audience—typically sitting near the first lady—whose stories illustrate policy goals. You'll remember the person's story more than the facts and figures that illustrate that person's case. Here's an example from President Obama's 2009 State of the Union:

> *I know that it is easy to lose sight of this truth—to become cynical and doubtful; consumed with the petty and the trivial.*
>
> *But in my life, I have also learned that hope is found in unlikely places; that inspiration often comes not from those with the most power or celebrity, but from the dreams and aspirations of Americans who are anything but ordinary. . . .*
>
> *I think about Greensburg, Kansas, a town that was completely destroyed by a tornado, but is being rebuilt by its residents as a global example of how clean energy can power an entire community—how it can bring jobs and businesses to a place where piles of bricks and rubble once lay. "The tragedy was terrible," said one of the men who helped them rebuild. "But the folks here know that it also provided an incredible opportunity." . . .*
>
> *We are not quitters.*[75]

If President Obama had just used his time to promote clean energy with facts and statistics, it would not have been memorable. However, by focusing on a town in the Midwest

# Step 10: Communicate the Results of Your Analysis

(which in general is a major source of energy from wind power), his message felt more immediate and personal. Note also that he ends with a very short, sound-bite sentence that clearly and concisely conveys his bottom-line message to the American people.

## How Should You Communicate Your Analysis?

Communicating your analysis is a two-step process. The first step is developing your message and the second step is disseminating your message so that it has impact.

The key fundamental principle of communication is that everyone's time is valuable and limited. As a result, your audience will make a choice—to read, watch, or listen to your message. You want to set yourself up for a positive outcome.

However, to be successful, you'll have to set aside some of the ways you have been taught to communicate in academic settings. Learn instead how to communicate in the "real world." In the end, it will likely benefit your scientific and technical writing as well.

### Developing Your Message

When developing your message to policymakers, you should keep in mind the following principles. Although the focus of this discussion is on writing, the same principles apply to recording a video or preparing a podcast about your policy ideas.

**Decide which communication methods to use for each audience.** Typically, in a policy context, you'll need to use multiple methods to reach your relevant audience—policymakers, stakeholders, and the general public. Appendix E provides some real-world examples from work I've done in West Virginia. Here are some options:

- **Policy Report:** Reports are where you provide detailed information on your policy analysis. This includes your data, analysis, findings, conclusions, and recommendations. Not all organizations, particularly government-related ones, will allow recommendations from their staff. The concept here is that it is up to the policymaker, not the staff, to decide on what to recommend after reviewing the data. On the other hand, you may well see recommendations from their advisory committees. You can see many examples of science and technology policy reports from the

National Academies of Sciences, Engineering, and Medicine;[76] RAND;[77] the Congressional Research Service;[78] academic policy centers; and other think tanks. Other examples are from federal advisory committees like the President's Council of Advisors on Science and Technology (PCAST)[79] and EPA's Science Advisory Board. These reports can be hundreds (and hundreds) of pages. A smaller version might be called a "white paper" or a "policymaker guide."

- **Policy Briefs:** Policy briefs are short documents that summarize the key messages of your report or focus on one issue. Ideally, they are one two-sided page (the "one-pager"). They can sometimes be longer. If it exceeds 10 pages, though, I question if it is a policy brief. They can be neutral (not making recommendations) or advocacy-oriented (encouraging specific actions). A one-pager policy brief is less than 1,000 words. I particularly like the ones put together by the United Nations Food and Agriculture Organization (FAO).[80] Appendix E has examples of policy briefs developed in consulting work I did for West Virginia University.

- **Policy Memos:** While policy briefs are intended for an external audience, policy memos are intended for an audience internal to your organization.[81] Here are two examples:

    - You believe that your university should take action to be more sustainable by eliminating all plastic food packaging on campus. The best way to communicate that message is to write a memo to the university president that presents the data and makes your case.

    - You are working for a policymaker and they ask you to put together a memo that summarizes and analyzes how to address inequities in flood insurance policy that are impacting constituents in your district given the new Biden Administration policy. They want you to identify possible policy options and make a recommendation.

    - Ideally, policy memos are a single one-sided page, but the person for whom you are writing the memo will typically provide guidance on how much detail they want. If you don't know the individual personally (as in the example of the university president), it's good to do some reconnaissance to find out what size of memos they like.

## Step 10: Communicate the Results of Your Analysis

- **Explainers:** Explainers are short documents that describe a key concept and provide background information and useful graphical descriptions for policymakers and the interested public. I particularly like the explainers produced by Resources for the Future, a think tank.[82] They actually produce them on a series of topics as two-pagers (four pages total) and sometimes as videos. A few sample topics from this think tank are "Social Cost of Carbon 101," "Gas Prices 101," and "Wildfires in the United States 101." Graphics are particularly helpful in keeping this kind of content clear, accessible, and interesting.

- **Science and Technology Notes:** Science and technology notes are somewhat like explainers and policy briefs, but they focus more on summarizing the academic literature. The legislative science notes developed for Missouri state legislators, for example, provide the highlights and limitations of rigorous, nonpartisan research as well as policy activities.[83]

- **Policy Elevator Pitch:** Say you're at a reception that includes national, state, or local policymakers. You want one of those policymakers to consider taking on your topic. The way you prepare for that event is to put together a 30-second or one-minute policy pitch.[84] In reality it will be a conversation with back-and-forth dialogue. The most important part is to start with your "ask"—what you want the policymaker to do about the societal challenge.

    You have to be quick, though, because the policymaker is certainly looking over your shoulder to see who else they should speak with at the event or if someone is heading your way to start their own pitch. So preparation is key to getting your policymaker's attention and hopefully getting a yes to your "ask"—probably a meeting with them or their staff to discuss the issue in more detail. Just keep in mind that all of the guidelines below about jargon, anecdotes, and so on also apply to verbal communication.

While you have control of the content of all of the above, you lose some of that control when you attempt to get your message out in a publication. Editors will typically have their own opinion on the focus of the article, the title, and so on. You give up a bit of control in exchange for access to the publication's audience. But published content can still be a great way to sway the public to your way of thinking. Consider options such as:

- **Policy Position Article:** This is an article that takes a point of view (POV) for an existing publication. Often called "perspectives" or "opinion" by publications, they are typically on the order of 1,500–2,000 words. You can find good examples of these in *Scientific American* and *Issues in Science and Technology*.[85]

- **Op-Eds:** Op-eds also present your POV in a publication, typically a newspaper or magazine. The length will vary depending on the publication, but 250–750 words is the norm. A variation is a letter to the editor, where you typically focus on providing your POV in response to an article in the newspaper. Getting an op-ed accepted is challenging but is certainly possible. The key is timeliness—why is that topic relevant *today*? The major newspapers that publish op-eds are the *New York Times* and the *Washington Post*, but state and local newspapers are also good candidates.

For all of the above, remember that a solid policy analysis is the core for all policy communications. To make your case, you need the analysis behind it. Otherwise, your opinion is no more interesting than anyone else's.

**Focus on your message, not on policy background or analytical methods.** The policymaker will trust your analysis, at least at the initial stage, so what they most want is to know your recommendation. All your more detailed analysis is best provided in a separate paper as opposed to the policymaking document.

You will need to break out of the mental model of a scientific paper, where you start from first principles and build to a conclusion. Even abstracts for scientific papers don't start with the core message first. Plus, abstracts will usually include your methods, which isn't useful for policy communication.

Instead you want to provide a story with a beginning, middle, and end. You also want to focus on the societal outcomes of your proposed policy (e.g., job creation), not the inputs (e.g., funding) or the outputs (e.g., technical worker training).

**Put your Bottom Line Up Front (BLUF).** The best way to think of Bottom Line Up Front (BLUF) communication is like a news article. When you're scanning a website, social media, or a newspaper, you read the headline first and then decide whether you're going to spend time reading the rest of the story. Even if you do click through, you may just read the first paragraph and not the full story. The same is true of policymakers. A well-constructed BLUF should be clear, concise, specific, and decisive, giving the policymaker a good understanding of the main message and the actions that need to be taken in a very limited period of time.

## Step 10: Communicate the Results of Your Analysis

Here's an example of where the bottom line is at the end, not the beginning:

> Artificial Intelligence (AI) is advancing at an unprecedented rate. This rapid progress has profound implications in numerous areas, including ethical standards, privacy issues, workforce education and development, and national security. Given these developments, it is crucial to create policies that ensure the balanced growth of AI technology while also protecting individual rights. Therefore, due to the rapid advancements in artificial intelligence, we recommend the immediate development and implementation of a comprehensive national AI policy that addresses these key areas.

In this case, the message starts by explaining the context (rapid advancements in AI) and the implications (impact on ethical standards, privacy, education, workforce development, and national security). It then concludes with the main point or "bottom line": the recommendation for the immediate development and implementation of a comprehensive national AI policy. This is the more traditional way of structuring arguments or recommendations, where you build up your points before delivering your conclusion or main message.

Here's an example where the bottom line is at the beginning, not the end:

> Due to the rapid advancements in artificial intelligence (AI), we recommend the immediate development and implementation of a comprehensive national AI policy. This policy should address key areas such as ethical guidelines, privacy protections, education and workforce development, and AI in national security to ensure balanced growth and safeguard individual rights.

This BLUF communicates the main message, which is the recommendation for the immediate development and implementation of a national AI policy due to rapid advancements in the field. The key areas that the policy should address are also summarized, giving a quick overview of the main points that the rest of the communication would likely elaborate upon.

From a policymaker perspective, they are primarily interested in the "ask"—so you want that at the very beginning, as in this case. If they're interested, they'll listen further. If you put the ask at the end, their attention might well wander.

**Don't use jargon.** Jargon terms are "the technical terminology or characteristic idiom of a special activity or group."[86] Scientists and engineers probably quite like that definition, but the alternative definitions are how the rest of the world sees them—"obscure and often pretentious language marked by circumlocutions and long words" and "confused unintelligible language."[87] My favorite jargon example is a word scientists use all the time—the word "model." Here are some differing definitions of the word "model" that illustrate how the word is viewed in different settings:

- a usually miniature representation of something (e.g., a plastic *model* of the human heart);

- a type or design of product (such as a car);

- a system of postulates, data, and inferences presented as a mathematical description of an entity or state of affairs; a computer simulation based on such a system (e.g., climate *model*);

- an example for imitation or emulation;

- one who is employed to display clothes or other merchandise; and

- a person or thing that serves as a pattern for an artist.[88]

You can imagine the confusion that might occur if you said something like "the model shows us that increased temperature will lead to increased precipitation," because your audience could easily be thinking about a fashion model, not "a computer simulation."

The table below, from the American Geophysical Union, provides a list of some other words related to climate change.[89] Just think about how you yourself use some of these words in your private life versus your professional life. A good example is the word "values." Consider someone reading it who doesn't live with your issue on a daily basis and so lacks the context to interpret what you're saying. You're thinking about numbers and they are thinking about ethics. They could probably do the same thing to you regarding their occupation and you would have the same difficulty. So always try to put yourself in their shoes as you write—and then have others who are not in science and technology read what you wrote and tell you where they feel confused or alienated.

## Step 10: Communicate the Results of Your Analysis

| Scientific Term | Public Meaning | Better Choice[89] |
|:---:|:---:|:---:|
| positive trend | good trend | upward trend |
| theory | hunch, speculation | scientific understanding |
| uncertainty | ignorance | range |
| error | mistake, wrong, incorrect | difference from exact true number |
| bias | distortion, political motive | offset from an observation |
| manipulation | illicit tampering | scientific data processing |
| sign | indication, astrological sign | plus or minus sign |
| values | ethics, monetary value | numbers, quantity |

Here's a list of questions to consider when thinking about your words:

1. What are three words/phrases you use regularly in your work that might be interpreted differently by those outside your field?

2. What are some alternatives you could use?

3. If you really need to use that word, what's a clear and memorable way to explain or define it?[90]

Also useful are "dejargonizer" tools where you can enter or upload text you have written and the words that are considered jargon are identified. These online tools are free to use.[91] Take a moment now to try out one of these tools on something you have written.

## Employ the 3Cs in Writing: Clear, Concise, and Coherent

When writing papers in academia, the content is rarely clear, concise, and coherent—at least to policymakers and the public. This is not the fault of the writer or the reader but rather the standards of academic writing. So to communicate effectively, you need to move into a "policy mindset" rather than an "academic mindset."

### Clear

Have you ever read the title or first few sentences of a written piece and then immediately put it down? Why did that happen? Perhaps it was incomprehensible and you thought: *I don't have time to figure out what this means, so I'm just not going to read it.*

Here's some advice from a university writing center on how to write clearly: "Choose the word that most clearly conveys your meaning. English words generally have two types of meanings: a denotative meaning (the descriptive dictionary definition of a word) and a connotative meaning (the emotional impact of a word). The connotation can be positive or negative. For example, the words slender, thin, and skinny all have the same denotative meaning, but very different connotations."[92]

Remember, policymakers focus on emotional impact. You can't influence your audience's emotions unless you've carefully considered your words' connotations—which may be different depending on audience factors such as demographics, location, and education.

For the second bullet, I can't tell you how many times I have written on a student's paper "What is 'this'?" As in "This is the reason you should support this policy." Too many uses of "this" will force your reader to flip back to previous paragraphs to figure out what you're talking about.

Speaking of writing centers, many universities have one. So if you are in an academic setting, take advantage of the guidance you can obtain there. When I was a professor at Carnegie Mellon University, they had a great writing center offering both seminars and private consultations that I would visit on occasion.

Everyone can benefit from someone else reading their writing. If you are not in an academic setting, consider having an editor read your work. Many freelance editors are available, or you might find an editor at your office willing to do a side gig. If you tell the individual guiding you that you are writing for policymakers, they can help you tailor your writing for that audience.

Step 10: Communicate the Results of Your Analysis

**Concise**
Academia can often give the impression that writing more is better than writing less. How many times have you been told to write a certain number of pages rather than focusing on the message? And imagine turning in a concise dissertation rather than one the size of a book! It would immediately be disparaged.

In the policy world, the opposite is true. Shorter is always better than longer. Policymakers are always short on time and need to gain a surface understanding of many issues. You are probably the same when it comes to your own professional reading activities. For example, think of yourself as a reader on a topic that interests you, but on which you are not an expert. Wouldn't you rather read a short, well-written (aka concise) article or even just a thoughtful headline or paragraph rather than a long book? Policymakers are the same—concise messages are much more likely to get their attention.

Writing less, however, is harder than writing more. You must think about every word. Does it really need to be there? Or are you providing far more detail than is needed? You'll have to cut that 20-word sentence to no more than 10 words. So it will take some practice to write concisely. Here's a useful list from a writing center:

- Eliminate unnecessary phrases and redundancies.
- Use clear and straightforward language.
- Write in an active voice.
- Shorten wordy phrases.
- Avoid starting sentences with "there is," "there are," or "it is."
- Eliminate extra nouns.
- Eliminate filler words such as "that," "of," or "up."[93]

**Coherent**
The word "coherent" means "logically or aesthetically ordered or integrated."[94] Coherent messages are consistent, understandable, and cohesive. For your message to be coherent, it needs to be jargon-free as discussed previously, but there also needs to be a logical flow. Your data should lead to your findings, which lead to your conclusion, which leads to your recommendation.

Keep in mind though that the BLUF philosophy mentioned earlier is important when communicating with policymakers. This logical flow linkage is more related to your analysis than your oral communication. You still need the logic with BLUF—it's just that the flow is backward rather than forward.

Always keep in mind that the more clear, concise, and coherent your message is, the more likely it is that a policymaker or member of the public will read it. This is not pleasure reading for them, nor is it required for them to read it. Your first goal is to get your audience to pick up that paper or click on that webpage. Following the 3Cs will get you to that goal.

**Employ the 3Rs in Speaking: Relevance, Real-World Impact, and Results**

Speaking is different from writing in some ways, but not in others. For example, you still need to keep in mind the 3Cs and BLUF as well as the 4Es, of course, but anecdotal evidence plays a greater role than data. Your presentation style also makes a difference. Here are some tips from Mark Bayer:

- **Give energy, get engagement:** Your level of enthusiasm drives audience attitudes. A droning talk gathers no supporters.

- **Identify and address stakeholder priorities:** Why should they care? Illustrate how your policymaker's constituents care about the topic (e.g., poll data). If the constituents care, the policymaker needs to care as well.

- **Start at the finish line:** Lead with the 3Rs: Relevance, Real-World Impact, and Results.
    - Relevance of proposed policies to their constituencies' concerns or priorities
    - Real-world application of policies to an illustrative constituent
    - Results the policies can achieve to benefit that constituent

- **Use content diversity:** Keep listeners' attention by varying your sentence structure, your gestures, and your speaking stance. Use rhetorical tools that motivate, persuade, or inform. For example, focus on a common myth (e.g., "Most PhDs work in academia," when in reality less than 50% do.[95]).

- **Remember primacy and recency:** Return to your most important point at the end to restate its relevance to listeners and emphasize the results they care about most.[96]

**Disseminating Your Message**

When your analysis is completed, you're only halfway there in terms of encouraging the implementation of your recommendation. Thinking about dissemination along the way

# Step 10: Communicate the Results of Your Analysis

is useful in working with other offices to plan for the release of your policy work along with follow-on activity.

In general, you want to build up what in marketing is called your "know, like, trust" factor. Policy and politics is built on personal relationships. You want to convey that you produce high-quality work and are approachable, likable, and trustworthy, as opposed to being self-centered, obnoxious, untrustworthy, and someone who produces shoddy work. Building a relationship doesn't happen overnight; it takes time.

|  | Know | Like | Trust |
|---|---|---|---|
| Goal | See your name and face many times | Appreciate your style | Be identified as someone people can count on |
| Do This | • Interact early and often with policymakers and stakeholders throughout your analysis to bring them into a co-creation process.<br>• Distribute content widely.<br>• Develop helpful and referrable content that users will quote and share with others. | • Be interesting and entertaining.<br>• Produce aspirational content to which your audience can relate.<br>• Provide a sense of empathy with your policymakers and stakeholders, particularly that you understand their challenges. | • Be consistent and authentic.<br>• Provide useful content over a long period of time.<br>• Respond quickly when called upon to convey information. |
| Not That | • Wait to interact with policymakers and stakeholders until after the analysis is completed.<br>• Let content "sit on the shelf," not distributing widely or often.<br>• Produce content that is not noteworthy, memorable, or referable. | • Be obnoxious, boring, rude, and portray a sense of superiority over your audience.<br>• Produce generic content that does not convey you or your personality or relate to your audience.<br>• Have a sense of entitlement that does not take into account your audience's challenges. | • Dismiss questions about your analysis and its uncertainties.<br>• Convey your information once without providing useful content to develop a long-term relationship.<br>• Take your time to respond without considering the needs of the policymakers. |

Ideally, you will have followed the steps outlined in this book to interact early and often with policymakers and stakeholders. That helps build up your "know, like, trust" factor so they are ready when you disseminate your message.

Below are the steps you should follow in developing your short- and long-term dissemination plan. Ideally, you should start developing your dissemination plan early in the process of conducting your policy analysis as you interact with policymakers and stakeholders.

**1. Make a list of people who constitute the audience for your message.**

Your audience list should include not only policymakers but stakeholders and the staff who would implement the recommended policy. It should also include what I call "carrier pigeons"—those who will help publicize your work through events, webinars, board meetings, and other places where you can interact with stakeholders and those who support your perspective. These "carrier pigeons" could include think tanks, foundations, universities, and nongovernmental organizations. Going back to our "ease of political acceptability" criterion, the more that key actors "know, like, trust" you, the more likely they are to help disseminate your message and support actions related to it.

**2. Develop a variety of dissemination products and events.**

Each of these audiences has different informational needs, as discussed earlier in this chapter. Or those needs might change over time. So while your policy analysis is the core of your work, you'll need to think about what you want to provide at each stage.

When meeting with a policymaker or their staff for the first time, a slide deck with your key points and your contact information is most useful. Then you can provide "leave-behinds"—the one-pager policy briefs described earlier. Finally, you can send a follow up email with links to the more in-depth work when you thank them for the meeting. This email also provides an opportunity to ask for their thoughts and perhaps request a future meeting to discuss an action like a hearing or co-sponsoring legislation.

Overall, you want to keep maintaining the relationship beyond that initial meeting. Further dissemination projects and information about your other work helps build that "like, know, trust" factor.

**3. Timing is important.**

You will have no impact on a policy if the major event for that policy has already

## Step 10: Communicate the Results of Your Analysis

occurred. So keep timing in mind as you identify events that can highlight your work, whether they're global, national, or local.

Examples include public events like Earth Day celebrations, historic events like the launch of Sputnik, major recurring legislation up for reauthorization such as the Farm Bill (which covers a lot more topics than farms!), and news events (like floods, hurricanes, and policymaker transitions). Also look for annual and board meetings of organizations, where you can advocate for getting on the agenda. Some public organizations, particularly federal advisory committees like the National Science Board and the President's Council of Advisors on Science and Technology Policy, even have a public comment period.

Prepare yourself to speak at these events by researching the views and backgrounds of those to whom you are speaking or communicating. For example, you can quickly embarrass yourself if you don't take the time to look at a policymaker's webpage to see what policies they have supported. Often, a policymaker will show that they're engaged in what you're saying by asking your opinion on parts of their own work that are similar to yours. Learning about a policymaker's personal background can also identify areas of commonality: perhaps you went to the same college or are interested in the same hobbies. For policies where you support their perspective, you can thank them for their work and show that you're engaged with them even outside your area of focus.

### Food Insecurity Example

As a reminder, here is the policy question we started with in Chapter 3:

> *What actions, if any, should the administrator at the U.S. Department of Agriculture Food and Nutrition Service (FNS) take to respond to equity concerns about federal nutrition assistance programs, particularly for households with children headed by a single woman that have the highest rate of food insecurity in the United States?*

In Chapter 4, we developed our policy options:

- Status quo: Households with children headed by a single woman have the highest rate of food insecurity. The Special Supplemental Nutrition Program for Women, Infants, and Children (WIC) helps pregnant women, mothers, and caregivers of infants and young children learn about good nutrition to keep themselves and their families healthy. The implementation of the program for current WIC participants is effective; however, only three out of five families eligible for the WIC program participate.

- Option 1: USDA's FNS should require WIC clinics to offer services over the phone and via video options and allow remote benefit issuance.

- Option 2: USDA's FNS should provide transportation vouchers to assist clients in going to WIC clinics.

And then we analyzed the effectiveness, efficiency, equity, and ease of political acceptability in Chapters 5–8. This resulted in this table in Chapter 9.

|  | Effectiveness | Efficiency | Equity | Ease of Political Acceptability |
|---|---|---|---|---|
| Status Quo: USDA WIC Program | − | − | − | ++ |
| Option 1: Digital application and benefits | + | ++ | ++ | + |
| Option 2: Transportation voucher | + | + | + | − |

As a result, we concluded that Option 1 was the best option:

- USDA's FNS should require WIC clinics to offer services over the phone and via video options and allow remote benefit issuance.

Now we are going to develop our policy brief title and policy elevator pitch. The policy brief title should begin with an action word, make clear the societal outcome, and be less than 10 words:

*Mandate Digital Application and Receipt of WIC Benefits*

## Step 10: Communicate the Results of Your Analysis

Now let's take that concept and turn it into an elevator policy pitch. We want to begin with the desired action and conclude with the societal benefit. In between, we want to fit in an anecdote and explain why it is important from a 4E perspective.

Here's a key point for Option 1 for each of the 4Es from the pro side in our 4E tables:

- **Effectiveness:** Study found that use of digital benefits increased participation by 8%.

- **Efficiency:** For each $1.00 spent on WIC services, Medicaid savings in costs for newborn medical care were $2.91. The benefits exceed the costs.

- **Equity:** Three groups with barriers to applying for WIC and receiving funds are those who have (1) transportation and other costs to reach WIC clinics; (2) language and clinical barriers; and (3) jobs where applying for services requires time away from work risking job loss and lost wages. All three of these groups with barriers would benefit from a digital registration option. This presumes that the website offers sufficient language options that they are no longer a barrier.

- **Ease of Political Acceptability:** Some states are already implementing this option.

We need to fit all four of these points into 30 seconds (about 100 words) to one minute (about 200 words), depending on the situation. Talking fast does *not* help with the 3Cs described earlier, so don't try to get your time down that way. We also don't want to fill our elevator pitch with data, because that's too hard to remember in the context of a conversation.

So now let's put together our one-minute policy pitch for our food insecurity example. Imagine that we are speaking with someone at an event and they have just asked us what we are working on these days. You respond:

**One-minute version**

> *USDA should require that WIC clinics provide digital methods to encourage the food insecure to apply and receive benefits. Did you know that households with children headed by a single woman have the highest rate of food insecurity? Yet about 40% of those eligible do not apply for WIC support because it is too challenging.*

*We met with Mary, a single mother of three children under the age of five, who only speaks Spanish. She doesn't have enough money for food, yet she is expected to apply in person for the program and then return monthly to get her benefits. This would cost her money for time off work or getting someone to take care of her kids. When she gets there, there might not be someone who can help her if they can't speak Spanish. So Mary has never registered for WIC, even though it would help her.*

*If she could apply and get her benefits with her mobile phone, however, as is the case in some states, she would participate. If a digital option was a nationwide requirement, then participation rates would increase, and hunger would decrease. Not only would we have less hunger, but society would save money because better nutrition leads to lower Medicaid costs.*

## 30-second version

*USDA should require that WIC clinics provide digital methods to encourage the food insecure to apply and receive benefits. Many eligible do not apply for WIC because in-person requirements can mean lost wages, childcare and transportation costs, and language barriers.*

*Mary, a single mother of three young children, doesn't have enough money for food, yet she is expected to apply and get her benefits in person.*

*If a digital option was a nationwide requirement, then WIC participation rates would increase. Not only would we have less hunger, but society would save money because better nutrition leads to lower Medicaid costs.*

### Tip: Making Public Policy Is Difficult and Time-Consuming

Making public policy is really difficult and can take a great deal of time—a decade is not uncommon. The table here comes from an article by Chris Tyler, who used to head the United Kingdom's version of the Congressional Research Service for science and technology, called POST, the Parliamentary Office of Science and Technology.

## Step 10: Communicate the Results of Your Analysis

### What You Should Know about Policymaking[97]

- Making policy is really difficult.
- No policy will ever be perfect.
- Policymakers can be experts too.
- Policymakers are not a homogenous group.
- Policymakers are people too.
- Policy decisions are subject to extensive scrutiny.
- Starting policies from scratch is very rarely an option.
- There is more to policy than scientific evidence.
- Public opinion matters.
- Policymakers do understand uncertainty.
- Policy and politics are not the same thing.
- Policy and science operate on different timescales.
- "We need more research" is the wrong answer.

Of particular note is that "no policy will ever be perfect"—that is because we cannot predict the future. Areas of uncertainty include both human behavior and world events such as pandemics, wars, and new knowledge and technologies that may come into play. It is also important to recognize that policymakers need to answer to their constituents. Those constituents are never just the scientific and technical community, but rather a host of individuals with different interests and cultural backgrounds. Public opinion does matter, so informing the public about your work is as important as informing policymakers.

Finally, why is "we need more research" the wrong answer? Policymakers need to make decisions now and cannot wait for more research to take action on a societal problem. So although research may be part of the answer, it is not a sufficient answer. Instead, policymakers make what we know are imperfect decisions and then modify those decisions as time goes on. One way to think about it is like peer review of research. We know that no research is the final answer or perfect, but over time the peer review process will identify errors and lead to new avenues of research that advance our understanding of our response to a given research question. Similarly, public policy will be updated over time as its practical application reveals its strengths and weaknesses.

## Thought Exercise 11: Develop Your One-Minute Policy Pitch

Develop your policy brief title and one-minute policy pitch for your recommendation. You'll find that both provide a good basis for the other communication products discussed in this chapter. You can, for example, use this information to pitch an op-ed or policy article to editors.

In addition, make sure you speak it out loud to a colleague. Verbal communication is different than written communication, and you'll find yourself making adjustments—typically making sentences much shorter and your messages much crisper. Also, don't attempt to race through your message. If you speak too fast, no one will be able to take in enough of your message to have a conversation about it, which is your ultimate goal.

_____
_____
_____
_____
_____
_____
_____
_____
_____

# Chapter 12: What's Next for Your Science and Technology Policy Journey?

Now that you've gained all this knowledge about science and technology policy, what's next? Many options for policy work are available throughout the United States and the world. A common assumption is that Washington, DC, is the only place to influence science and technology policy. Nothing is further from the truth. You can start out in the town, city, or state where you live and be just as successful in informing and influencing policymakers with your scientific and technical knowledge.

## Ways to Inform and Influence Policymakers

Here are some ideas on ways to inform and influence policymakers about societal opportunities and challenges you care about:

- **Speak at a policymaker event.** Opportunities to make a brief comment as part of public meetings are common at all levels of government. You can make a statement about a current policy or propose new policies.

- **Provide written comments on a proposed policy.** A law may already be passed, but it is the executive branch that handles implementation. Often they make requests for comments on draft policies or requests for information. A thoughtful response can have a substantive impact on a policy headed the wrong way.

- **Serve on a board or commission.** Many boards and commissions, particularly at the local level, lack any scientific or technical expertise. Investigate how you can join or be appointed to the one in your community.

- **Run for political office.** Who says you can't run for political office yourself? There are even organizations focused on providing the training and support so more scientists, engineers, and health professionals are ready to run for office at all levels of government.

You can also focus on partnering with others who share your same ideals and who could use some scientific and technical support. This is particularly true for nongovernmental organizations (NGOs). Just look for organizations in your area of interest and ask them how you can get involved.

Another option is to participate in one of the many fellowship programs that are available for scientists, engineers, and health professionals. The most well-known program is that of the American Association for the Advancement of Science (AAAS), but an increasing number of states have similar programs, and many science and engineering disciplinary societies, foundations, and other organizations have their own programs. In addition, there are state and local programs as well as those focused on specific topics.

Federal, state, and local agencies also have fellowships and internships that are focused on particular topics. If you are at the middle or senior level, you can also seek one of the programs where you provide your services to a federal agency for a year or two through the Intergovernmental Personnel Act.

Perhaps you prefer to be a solo practitioner of science and technology policy. There are still opportunities to write op-eds and articles, speak up at local events, and analyze data so that it is useful for others.

So, opportunities abound! Which one is right for you?

## What Are Common Obstacles to Having a Societal Impact and How Can You Overcome Them?

Here are the top mistakes I see when scientists, engineers, and health professionals communicate with policymakers.

### Unclear "ask".

An unclear "ask" occurs when you explain the societal problem you want the policymaker to address and the results of your analysis, perhaps even going as far as making a recommendation, but then you don't tell the policymaker what concrete action you want them to take next.

Instead, specify what next step you want the policymaker to take. Is it to introduce legislation, hold a hearing, host a meeting with key stakeholders to discuss your idea, or have staff evaluate the idea so it can be discussed in a future meeting with you?

| Action Category | Action Examples[98] |
|---|---|
| Legislative | Introduce new legislation; cosponsor existing legislation; offer an amendment to existing legislation; and make a floor statement. |
| Committees | Hold hearings; ask specific questions of witnesses at or after hearings; include specific report language with a bill leaving a committee; request appropriations language; and support or oppose a nominee for an official appointment to an executive position, board, or similar politically appointed position. |
| Oversight | Write letters to agency heads; ask for briefings from agency staff; and comment on proposed legislation. |
| Partner | Join a sign-on letter; organize a briefing for elected officials or staff; and join an issue-focused caucus. |
| External | Give a speech or attend an event; and issue a press release. |

**Not researching your audience and their position on your issue.**

There is nothing more embarrassing than meeting with a policymaker's staff and hearing them say, "What did you think of the bill our member of Congress introduced on the issue?" if you didn't already know about that bill. They may also mention a speech they made, legislation they cosponsored, a hearing they held, and so on.

Take the time to research your targeted policymaker. Information about policymakers' past achievements is typically available online, including their website, websites of the committees on which they serve, and news articles.

As mentioned earlier, you should also look for commonalities between you and the policymaker and their family (e.g., you went to the same college, or grew up in the same town) to help establish a connection with that policymaker. It would be somewhat embarrassing if they mention they went to your high school or university, for example, and you did not know that information.

Finally, you may need to understand the policymaker's constituencies and their position on the issue at hand. For example, if there is a major national laboratory, university, or research institute, you need to know who is active on the issue there and what position or research papers they have written on the issue. Demographic data (like unemployment rates and the like) and poll data relevant to your issue, if available, is also useful.

**Making assumptions about or looking down on policymakers and their staff.**

A frequent mistake I see scientists and engineers make when talking to policymakers is assuming that all policymakers who belong to a particular political party have the same position on all issues. They might think, for example, that all Republicans oppose action on climate change[99] or that all Democrats support abortion rights.[100] This is not the case. As one senior senator told me once, "It's the person, not the party." This is particularly true on many science and technology policy issues.

Another mistake I see is that sometimes people who have STEM degrees think they are smarter than others, that they know more, are making more of a contribution to society, and so on. This thinking is not uncommon for members of any profession. Even within STEM, physicists may think they are better than biologists, biologists think they are better than social scientists, scientists think they are better than engineers, and so forth.

The challenge is when those attitudes come through to policymakers and their staff such that they give an "ivory tower" view of the world. An ivory tower is defined as "an impractical, often escapist attitude marked by aloof lack of concern with or interest in practical matters or urgent problems."[101]

Instead, recognize that each policymaker is an individual person and don't make assumptions about their positions on issues. Furthermore, everyone has their own area of expertise, and while yours may be STEM, policymakers know how to make policy happen. This is also true for members of the public: they know their community the best, and talking down to them is the best way to alienate them and lose the benefit of all they know.

For example, I once invited a senior scientist to present the results from a committee report to key White House Office of Science and Technology Policy staff. The scientist spent about half the time talking about the importance of acting on climate change—that was wasted time. These individuals, part of the Obama Administration, already knew action was necessary and probably even had more sense of urgency than the senior scientist did. As a result, the top officials started to drift out of the room, one by one. Then the senior scientist left no time for questions, instead speaking for all but 10 minutes. Everyone at that point had to leave for the next meeting, and this became a lost opportunity for a true discussion of the proposals developed by the committee.

The best way you can create a genuine dialogue is by being a respectful listener more than a talker, so you understand policymakers' challenges and concerns regarding your proposed policy. You can do this by limiting the amount you speak to no more than 40% of the time scheduled and keeping the remaining 60% of the time for discussion. Further, rather than a classic PowerPoint presentation, make it more of a dialogue. People will need to come and go. You need to leave time for discussion as you go along, so both parties can benefit from the meeting.

## Gaining a Policy Mindset

By reading this book and implementing the exercises within it, you are now on your way to gaining a policy mindset. Through this policy mindset, you will be able to take a broader look at the societal challenges we face and develop policy solutions that don't just focus on effectiveness, but also consider other factors such as efficiency, equity, and ease of political acceptability.

You also now understand the difference between "science and technology for policy" and "policy for science and technology." And even more importantly, you see how interactions with policymakers differ depending on whether your focused on "policy for S&T" or "S&T for policy." Further, you recognize that interactions with stakeholders are necessary throughout your analysis, not just at the end when you're presenting your recommendations.

You've learned how to communicate clearly to policymakers and the public by putting your Bottom Line Up Front, using anecdotes to illustrate your points, and avoiding jargon. And when communicating, you know to make sure that you understand the timing of the policy of interest—not presenting your analysis after the decisions have already been made, but at a time when you can be part of the policymaking process.

You've learned how to avoid common obstacles, such as an unclear "ask," not knowing enough about the policymakers you're talking to, making assumptions about policymakers' positions, and the importance of listening to policymakers rather than looking down on them from an ivory tower.

The appendices provide additional information, including thinking about how you want to engage with policymakers (Appendix B) and the challenges you may face when you do so (Appendix C). I've also provided resources (Appendix D) and organizations you can join so you can interact with others who are interested in science and technology policy, just like you.

Finally, you now are aware of the many opportunities to get involved in policymaking. What will you choose? Let me know by visiting the [Science and Technology Policy Academy website](#) and telling me your story. I'm ready and eager to listen!

# THE BEST WAY TO THANK AN AUTHOR IS TO POST A REVIEW ON AMAZON!

# Appendix A: Brief History of Science and Technology Policy in the United States

The beginnings of science and technology policy (S&T) in the United States, both "policy for science" and "science for policy," go back to the founding of the United States. Founding fathers, including Benjamin Franklin, Thomas Jefferson, Alexander Hamilton, John Adams, James Madison, and George Washington, had significant interest in scientific fields and were key to making sure science got mentioned in the Declaration of Independence and the Constitution. That said, according to one scholar,[102] the founders did not envision the U.S. government as the primary source of funding for U.S. research and development, nor were they able to reach an agreement on the need for a national university.

Nevertheless, one can see several scientific, engineering, mathematical, and health principles that influenced the development of the United States. The U.S. Declaration of Independence (1776), as penned by Thomas Jefferson, includes key phrases such as "laws of nature" (Newton's laws[103]) and "truths to be self-evident" (Euclid's axioms[104]).

> **Declaration of Independence Excerpt (emphasis added)**
>
> The unanimous Declaration of the thirteen united States of America, When in the Course of human events, it becomes necessary for one people to dissolve the political bands which have connected them with another, and to assume among the powers of the earth, the separate and equal station to which the **Laws of Nature** and of Nature's God entitle them, a decent respect to the opinions of mankind requires that they should declare the causes which impel them to the separation.
>
> We hold these **truths to be self-evident**, that all men are created equal, that they are endowed by their Creator with certain unalienable Rights, that among these are Life, Liberty and the pursuit of Happiness.

# Appendix A: Brief History of Science and Technology Policy in the United States

Although these words are credited to Thomas Jefferson, in reality Jefferson indicated he "adopted the 'harmonizing sentiments of the day'"[105] from the era of Enlightenment Enlightenment (aka Age of Reason) discussed throughout Western civilization.

Beyond the Declaration of Independence, we see the need for science and engineering in the Constitution (1787), which identifies the need for patent and copyright laws, developing standards of weights and measures (important in a day when gold and other materials were used to make coins), and conducting a population census (as a basis for a direct tax):

> "[The Congress shall have Power . . . ] To coin Money, regulate the Value thereof, and of foreign Coin, and fix the Standard of Weights and Measures" [U.S. Constitution, Article I, Section 8, Clause 5]

> "To promote the Progress of Science and useful Arts, by securing for limited Times to Authors and Inventors the exclusive Right to their respective Writings and Discoveries" [U.S. Constitution, Article I, Section 8, Clause 8]

> "No Capitation, or other direct, Tax shall be laid, unless in Proportion to the Census or enumeration herein before directed to be taken." [U.S. Constitution, Article I, Section 9, Clause 4]

Other key players from the scientific, engineering, and medical communities brought their skills to respond to the nation's needs throughout U.S. history. Examples include inventor and astronomer David Rittenhouse, who designed telescopes used by the army and was the first director of the U.S. mint; physician and chemist Benjamin Rush, who was the country's first surgeon general and promoted public health; and Charles Wilson Peale, who organized the nation's first natural history scientific expedition. Later we see the Lewis and Clark expedition (1803–1806, aka Corps of Discovery Expedition), commissioned by Thomas Jefferson, to explore the natural world beyond the original 13 colonies. These leaders represent only a small number of the many scientists who formed the basis of today's American S&T policy.

Prior to World War II, most research and development (R&D) activities were funded and conducted by the private sector, including universities, foundations, businesses, and industries. This changed during World War II as the government made major investments in R&D. The biggest investment was the Manhattan Project, where the government hired scientists and engineers to develop and manufacture the first atomic bomb.

Following World War II, Vannevar Bush, director of the Office of Scientific Research and Development, developed a report for President Franklin D. Roosevelt about the role science, engineering, and health professionals should play in the government. This report, called Science: The Endless Frontier remains the basis for today's science and technology policy and led to the establishment of the National Science Foundation. One of the report's key points was that "Scientific Progress Is Essential," stating:

> *Progress in the war against disease depends upon a flow of new scientific knowledge. New products, new industries, and more jobs require continuous additions to knowledge of the laws of nature, and the application of that knowledge to practical purposes. Similarly, our defense against aggression demands new knowledge so that we can develop new and improved weapons. This essential, new knowledge can be obtained only through basic scientific research.*
>
> *The Government should accept new responsibilities for promoting the flow of new scientific knowledge and the development of scientific talent in our youth. These responsibilities are the proper concern of the Government, for they vitally affect our health, our jobs, and our national security. It is in keeping also with basic United States policy that the Government should foster the opening of new frontiers and this is the modern way to do it. For many years the Government has wisely supported research in the agricultural colleges and the benefits have been great. The time has come when such support should be extended to other fields.*
>
> *Science can be effective in the national welfare only as a member of a team, whether the conditions be peace or war. But without scientific progress no amount of achievement in other directions can insure our health, prosperity, and security as a nation in the modern world.*[106]

Following the report, government scientists, engineers, and mathematicians began to play a role in responding to societal needs in all fields of science and technology. Mollie Orshansky, a government mathematician and statistician, developed the way we measure poverty. Rear Admiral Grace Murray Hopper developed ways to ease the processing and programming of data that provided a way for more evidence-based policy. Katherine Johnson, a mathematics leader at the National Aeronautics and Space Administration, served a similar role by analyzing flight and spacecraft test data to enhance the safety of astronauts and passengers. Mary Engle Pennington developed the standards we use for processing and refrigeration so we have safe foods to eat.

# Appendix B: How Do You Want to Engage with Policymakers?

Roger Pielke, in his book *The Honest Broker: Making Sense of Science in Policy and Politics*, identifies what he calls the four idealized modes of engagement between scientists and policy/politics.[107] As illustrated in the figure seen below, he breaks down the view of science in society into two models. The first, the linear model, takes the perspective that science can change public opinion, which in turn can change the direction of public policy. This differs from the stakeholder model, in which both scientists and the public work to understand each other's perspectives, resulting in the co-production of knowledge.

He also incorporates different views of democracy. Interest group pluralism is the perspective that policymaking results from interest groups competing with each other. Elite conflict is when those with knowledge and expertise (in this case) disagree with each other.

This results in four idealized modes of engagement: Pure Scientist, Issue Advocate, Science Arbiter, and Honest Broker of Policy Alternatives. So the science arbiter, for example, plays the role of resolving conflict among the scientific and technical community, which can change public opinion, which in turn will influence the direction of public policy.

| Four Idealized Modes of Engagement | | |
|---|---|---|
| **View of Democracy** | **View of Science in Society** | |
| | Linear Model | Stakeholder Model |
| Interest Group Pluralism | Pure Scientist | Issue Advocate |
| Elite Conflict | Science Arbiter | Honest Broker of Policy Alternatives |

Source: Roger Pielke Jr., Five Modes of Science Engagement, blog, January 19, 2015.[106]

Here's my spin on each (which is a bit different from Dr. Pielke's, which is provided briefly in parentheses). As you read each, think about what category you yourself, as well as your colleagues, fall into:

- **Pure scientist (no engagement)**: This is the individual who just wants to do their research and has no interest in policy. Those at the extreme level may resent that some federal agencies require that they show the broader impacts and social relevance of their work to get funding for their research. They might also go so far as to make derogatory comments about those who engage in policy, discourage their graduate students and postdocs from engaging in public policy, and downgrade those who engage in policy when reviewing them for tenure.

- **Issue advocate (reduce choice to preferred outcome[s])**: This individual feels so strongly about one specific issue that they participate in advocacy groups, protests, and other events. The issue on which they are advocating may or may not be within their particular area of expertise. At the extreme they may care so much about their issue that they may be unwilling to consider analysis that is contrary to their personal views.

- **Science arbiter (provide answers to questions with empirical answers)**: Science arbiters aim to bring together the consensus of the S&T community on the issue at hand. The key examples for this are federal advisory committees managed by federal agencies and the study committees of the National Academies of Sciences, Engineering, and Medicine. At the extremes, the goal of consensus is so strong that the result may be the lowest common denominator, as opposed to the most appropriate result based on analysis. Another challenge is the influence of staff, particularly on federal advisory committees, in identifying the study question and choosing the committee members.

- **Honest broker of policy alternatives (clarify and expand scope of options available for action)**: The goal of honest brokers is to expand the perception of policymakers to understand the array of options available and to then analyze those options in a neutral manner. At the extremes, they may be "too neutral"—so much so that the policymaker is still uncertain as to what action to take based on expert advice.

## Appendix B: How Do You Want to Engage with Policymakers?

In general, if you're a pure scientist, it's unlikely that you are reading this book. Research may be the focus of your day-to-day activities, but this is a book about policy, and if you're reading it you are at least somewhat interested in public policy and the role your expertise might play in it. I often find that my students view themselves as issue advocates today, but think they will be science arbiters or honest brokers in the future.

Why does determining your mode of engagement with policymakers matter? As with the discussion of "policy for S&T" and "S&T for policy," this influences how policymakers view you when you talk or meet with them. It also relates to how you present your scientific and technical knowledge to policymakers. If, for example, you're an issue advocate, you'll tend to focus on all the reasons why the policymaker should take action and your response to those who oppose action. On the other hand, if you're an honest broker, you will provide the policymaker with a number of options for action (including no action at all) and the pros and cons of each. Further, while you might recommend an action, you are not saying a particular action is the only one to take.

# Appendix C: Challenges You May Face in Bringing Your Expertise to Policymaking

Bringing scientific and technical evidence to policymakers is not without its challenges. So you should keep that in mind when you begin this journey into S&T Policy. Here are some real-world recent examples to inspire you, should you face similar challenges.

In the 1960s, Frances Oldham Kelsey, a researcher in the U.S. Food and Drug Administration, refused to approve the use of the drug thalidomide. Thalidomide was widely used in Europe, and there was a lot of pressure to approve it in the U.S. Kelsey, however, maintained that there wasn't enough evidence that the drug was safe—and she was right. Her decision saved countless babies from birth defects.[108] In the end, she was awarded the President's Medal for Distinguished Service by President Kennedy.

You may also have learned in your high school years about Rachel Carson, whose 1962 book *Silent Spring* led to the banning of DDT. She faced many detractors at the time, including one who said, "Her book is more poisonous than the pesticides she condemns."[109]

We've seen examples of policymakers attacking scientists during the COVID-19 pandemic when Dr. Anthony Fauci, director of the National Institute of Allergy and Infectious Diseases (NIAID) at the National Institutes of Health (NIH), was attacked personally, and even received death threats, after making statements about the pandemic and the appropriate response. His response illustrates the common perspective I've seen when scientific and technical leaders are speaking "truth to power":

> *Attacks on me, quite frankly, are attacks on science. All of the things I have spoken about, consistently, from the very beginning, have been fundamentally based on science. Sometimes those things were inconvenient truths for people.*[110]

Even prior to these attacks, Maria McNutt, president of the National Academy of Sciences, and Victor J. Dzau, president of the National Academy of Medicine, felt compelled to make a joint statement in 2020:

# Appendix C: Challenges You May Face in Bringing Your Expertise to Policymaking

*As advisers to the nation on all matters of science, medicine, and public health, we are compelled to underscore the value of science-based decision-making at all levels of government. Our nation is at a critical time in the course of the COVID-19 pandemic with important decisions ahead of us, especially concerning the efficacy and safety of vaccines.*

*Policymaking must be informed by the best available evidence without it being distorted, concealed, or otherwise deliberately miscommunicated. We find ongoing reports and incidents of the politicization of science, particularly the overriding of evidence and advice from public health officials and derision of government scientists, to be alarming. It undermines the credibility of public health agencies and the public's confidence in them when we need it most.*

*Ending the pandemic will require decision-making that is not only based on science but also sufficiently transparent to ensure public trust in, and adherence to, sound public-health instructions. Any efforts to discredit the best science and scientists threaten the health and welfare of us all.*[111]

Interestingly, an academic study of conflicts between science and policy found that both conservatives and liberals frequently disagree with scientists on key issues. So don't presume that politicians of either party will not challenge your thinking. This table[112] provides an overview.

| | |
|---|---|
| Conservatives are likely to object to the strong scientific consensus on . . . | Embryonic stem cell research, climate change, childhood obesity and diet restrictions, coal production regulation, and teaching evolution |
| Liberals are likely to object to the strong scientific consensus on . . . | Biotech food and crops, animal testing for medical research, and mandatory childhood vaccination |

The goal of this book is to teach you how to be an honest broker of policy alternatives. I think this is the best option to have as a core skill set for whatever role you take in S&T policy. If you are an issue advocate, for example, your work will be strengthened by understanding why some might oppose the policy for which you are advocating. You will then be prepared to present a counterargument or negotiate with those who oppose the policy for which you are advocating. If you work in a position where you are playing the role of a science arbiter, then you should be able to present the pros and cons of actions to the experts with whom you are working. They may know the scientific and technical evidence related to the effectiveness of a policy, but they frequently lack knowledge of issues related to the efficiency, equity, or ease of political acceptability related to the actions they are considering.

Although I consider myself an honest broker today, I have played all of these roles in my S&T policy career at different stages. During my 20s, I was an issue advocate with the League of Women Voters in Texas, serving as the president of a local league and on the state board of directors. At that point, I was lobbying for container deposit legislation (where you pay a nickel when you buy a can of soda and then get that nickel back when you recycle it). During my early 30s, while earning my PhD, I was a pure scientist, focused on producing knowledge to understand better the role of science played in international environmental agreements. For the decades after that, particularly in my 18 years at the NASEM and three years at the White House, I was a science arbiter, providing analysis that supported expert committee members bringing their expertise to bear on a societal challenge facing the nation. In between, I was an honest broker while working for the Congressional Research Service.

In the end, I think it's important to understand what role you are playing at a particular moment in time. No role is better or worse than another—they are just different players in the ever-fascinating world of S&T policy.

# Appendix D: Resources

You will find many useful resources on the Science and Technology Policy Academy's website and YouTube page. Provided below are some illustrative resources.

For those of you who are interested in a more traditional academic perspective on some of the topics in this book, here is a reading list:

- E. Bardach and E. Patashnik, *A Practical Guide for Policy Analysis: The Eightfold Path to More Effective Problem Solving*, 6th ed., July 2019. This guide is designed for public policy analysis students. I've been using it for decades because it's short, written in a nonacademic fashion, and practical, so it is well suited for science, engineering, and health professionals interested in public policy analysis. Earlier editions are fine and it is frequently available in digital form at university libraries.

- Granger M. Morgan, *Theory and Practice in Policy Analysis : Including Applications in Science and Technology*. Granger Morgan was the person who hired me as a professor of the practice in engineering and public policy at Carnegie Mellon University. During my first year there, I observed his classes as often as I could while he was in the process of writing this book. He's the best person I know who is able to make the connection between theory and practice (as indicated in the title). If you're looking at producing journal articles focused on science and technology policy, particularly those with original data to analyze, this is the book for you.

- Paul Cairney, *Politics and Public Policy*, a professor of politics and public policy at the University of Stirling in Scotland, has a useful webpage where he presents politics and public policy theory in 500-, 750-, and 1,000-word chunks. So if you are someone who likes to know the theory behind what I've presented in this book (which intentionally does *not* cover theory), I recommend this page.

For those interested in resources from practitioners in the field, here are some useful publications, videos, and websites:

- E. Suhay, E. Cloyd, E. Heath, and E. Nash, Recommended Practices for Science Communication with Policymakers.
- Broad Research Communication Lab, Public Policy Communication.
- Compass, The Message Box. If your focus is on presenting just your research to policymakers, Compass provides this useful tool.
- Beyond Sputnik: U.S. Science Policy in the 21st Century. Although now somewhat dated, if you are interested in policy for science, this book is still a useful resource.
- American Geophysical Union, Science Policy
- Conservation Strategy Fund, Cost-Benefit Analysis
- Engineers and Scientists Acting Locally, Playbook

There are many career guides and opportunities available for scientists, engineers, and health professionals seeking to enter public policy. Here are two:

- Science Policy: A Guide to Policy Careers for Scientists. This is a career guide developed by alumni of the California Council on Science and Technology Policy fellowship program.

- National Science Policy Network. NSPN has lots of activities that are focused on teaching and providing opportunities for early career scientists and engineers to engage in policymaking.

While policy is the substance of what is being decided, politics is the process of how those decisions are made. This book focuses on evidence-based policymaking, not politics. To enhance your understanding of U.S. national politics, I suggest that you watch a popular show from the past called West Wing. I've watched this show many times over the decades since it came out, and it still rings true as to "how the sausage is made." You will likely be surprised at how recurring the issues are. The advisors were former White House officials and you can see the evidence of their understanding in the work. I still use excerpts from the show when I am teaching workshops and classes.

# Appendix E: West Virginia Carbon Dioxide Reduction Example

For the past several years, I have worked with West Virginia University's Bridge Initiative for Science and Technology Policy, Leadership, and Communications as a consultant. My primary task is working as a study director, in partnership with their faculty, to develop policymaker guides and related products such as policy briefs.

To see an illustration of "real-world" analysis, go to https://scitechpolicy.wvu.edu/ and take a look at a policymaker guide entitled "Carbon Dioxide and West Virginia: A Science and Technology Perspective." You will also see related dissemination activities including policy briefs, science and technology notes, and webcasts.

While reviewing the policymaker guide, look for the following:

1. **Statement of Work:** Note the use of the "What actions, if any" question model and the discussion of stakeholder input.

2. **Timeline of Activities:** Note the stakeholder roundtables.

3. **Roundtables:** Overview of the roundtable discussion.

4. **Opportunities and Challenges Tables:** This is a policymaker version of the 4E pro/con table illustrated throughout this guide. "Science and Technology" is "effectiveness," "Economic Prosperity" is "efficiency," and "Environment and Conservation Impact" is "equity." In this study, consideration of "Disadvantaged Communities" is a combination of "equity" and "ease of political acceptability." That is because the people impacted are part of issues related to fairness, but they can also object to hosting direct air capture, for example, in their neighborhoods. Without their support, direct air capture is unlikely to occur in these communities. These communities were selected as possible locations for direct air capture because they are some of the poorest in West Virginia, and while economic development can help create jobs, residents are likely to also be worried about the possible environmental impact.

## About the Author

Dr. Deborah D. Stine is the founder of the Science and Technology Policy Academy.

She is a freelance consultant, policy analyst, writer, keynote and workshop speaker, leadership and career coach, and study director whose career has been dedicated to translating science and technology to policymakers, the public, students, and investors—*and* translating policymakers, the public, students, and investors to the science and technology community.

She was executive director of the President's Council of Advisors on Science and Technology (PCAST) at the White House from 2009 to 2012, during the first three years of the Obama Administration. During that time, she was the study director on a wide variety of science and technology policy topics, including advanced manufacturing, spectrum allocation, influenza vaccine production, nanotechnology, networking and information technology, ecosystems and the economy, and STEM education that led to Obama Administration initiatives.

## About the Author

At Carnegie Mellon, Dr. Stine was a professor of the Practice for the Engineering and Public Policy Department and associate director for Policy Outreach for the Scott Institute for Energy Innovation from 2012 to 2018. Dr. Stine received the Carnegie Science Communication Award for her communication activities, particularly videos, for her work at Carnegie Mellon.

From 2007 to 2009, she was a science and technology policy specialist with the Congressional Research Service. There she wrote reports on many topics, including a comparison of the Apollo program, Manhattan Project, and Energy Research and Development programs; science and technology diplomacy; and a primer on science and technology policy, ARPA-E, and the America COMPETES Act.

From 1989 to 2007, she was at the National Academies of Sciences, Engineering, and Medicine, where she was associate director of the Committee on Science, Engineering, and Public Policy; director of the National Academies Christine Mirzayan Science and Technology Policy Fellowship Program; and director of the Office of Special Projects. While there, she received the highest staff award from the National Academies. She was the study director for the *Rising Above the Gathering Storm* report that led to the America COMPETES Act and the establishment of the Advanced Research Projects Agency-Energy (ARPA-E).

Prior to coming to the academies, she was a mathematician for the Air Force, an air-pollution engineer for the state of Texas, and an air-issues manager for the Chemical Manufacturers Association. She was also president of the League of Women Voters of Corpus Christi and a member of the league's Texas Board of Directors.

Dr. Stine was elected a Fellow of the American Association of the Advancement of Science "for her major, long-term contributions to national science and technology policy and the development of the science and technology policy workforce of the future." She received a Carnegie Science Communication award for her ability to explain complex scientific and technical information to policymakers and the public.

Dr. Stine holds a BS in mechanical and environmental engineering from the University of California, Irvine, an MBA from what is now Texas A&M at Corpus Christi, and a PhD in public administration with a focus on science and technology policy analysis from American University.

# About the Science and Technology Policy Academy

The Science and Technology Policy Academy is for scientists, engineers, and health professionals who are serious about a career in science and technology policy. The academy offers on-demand and live classes, workshops for organizations, executive and career coaching, and "done for you" policy analysis, program evaluation, and policymaker and public communication services.

The academy teaches or coaches students and professionals on the fundamentals of science and technology policy and careers, and how to analyze science- and technology-related issues using policy analysis, benefit-cost analysis, and other techniques. Students and professionals can take classes independently or through organizations like universities, disciplinary societies, and student groups.

The Science and Technology Policy Academy's "Done for You" services can develop science and technology policy-related analysis and communication products and services, including gathering information from experts and stakeholders.

You can go to the S&T Policy Academy website at www.scitechpolicyacademy.com to sign up for the monthly newsletter, where you will hear about free workshops and webinars as well as classes you can take to bring your skills to the next level. If you sign up for the email list, you will get access to a free fillable PDF version of the book where you can fill in your responses to the thought activities.

# Endnotes

1 American Society for Microbiology, "How Microbes Clean up Oil: Lessons From the Deepwater Horizon Oil Spill," April 19, 2020.

2 National Academies of Sciences, Engineering, and Medicine. *Science and Judgment in Risk Assessment*, 1994.

3 Organization for Economic Cooperation and Development (OECD), *Science, Growth, and Society: A New Perspective*, 1971; known as the "Brooks report" after Harvey Brooks, the chair of the panel that developed this report.

4 National Academies of Sciences, Engineering, and Medicine, *Policy Implications of Greenhouse Warming: Mitigation, Adaptation, and the Science Base*, 1992.

5 Science, "Realistic Mitigation Options for Global Warming," July 10, 1992.

6 National Academies of Sciences, Engineering, and Medicine, *Rising Above the Gathering Storm: Energizing and Employing America for a Brighter Economic Future*, 2005 (prepublication), 2007 (final publication).

7 J-PAL, "Microcredit: Impacts and promising innovations," May 2023.

8 Hesketh, T., & Zhu, W. X. (1997). "The one child family policy: The good, the bad, and the ugly." *BMJ : British Medical Journal*, 314(7095), 1685-1687.

9 *National Geographic*, "How China's One-Child Policy Backfired Disastrously," October 30, 2015.

10 These steps are a more in-depth version of the steps provided by Bardach and Patashnik in their book, *A Practical Guide for Policy Analysis: The Eightfold Path to More Effective Problem Solving*.

11 The original concept of something like the 4Es comes from David Weimer and Adam Vining in their textbook *Policy Analysis: Concepts and Practice*. I (and others) have modified their original concepts over time.

12 Abraham Lincoln, "Fragment on Government," 1854.

13 Apple, "Apple calls on global supply chain to decarbonize by 2030," Apple Newsroom, October 25, 2022.

14 "24% of Harvard families pay nothing for their students to attend." Admissions & Financial Aid, accessed December 20, 2023.

15 "[Undergraduate families under $100,000 income to pay no tuition, room, or board at Stanford beginning in 2023-24](#)," Stanford Report, February 9, 2023.

16 California Institute for Regenerative Medicine, "[History-CIRM](#)," Accessed December 20, 2023.

17 CBS News (Moneywatch), "[Nearly a quarter of U.S. adults sometimes don't get enough to eat](#)," March 21, 2023.

18 Feeding America, "[Facts about child hunger in America](#)," accessed July 14, 2023.

19 [USDA Economic Research Service](#), 2021.

20 Baltimore Hunger Project, "[Root Causes of Poverty in the United States and Baltimore](#)," 2020.

21 [White House Conference on Hunger, Nutrition, and Health](#), September 2022.

22 Ibid.

23 [NOAA Fisheries](#), 2022.

24 Food Safety News, "[Report: 'Bycatch' Blamed for Nine Dirty Ocean Fisheries Off U.S. Shores](#)," 2014.

25 United Nations World Food Programme, [Women and WFP: Helping Women Help Themselves](#), March 2011.

26 Charity Charge, "[10 Impactful Food Organizations Tackling Hunger and Food Insecurity](#)," accessed December 2022.

27 *The Economist*, [Global Food Security Index 2022](#), accessed December 2022.

28 Bloomberg, "[Ireland Tops U.S. as the Country Best Able to Feed Its People](#)," September 26, 2017.

29 *The Journal* (Dublin), "[Opinion: The last year should teach us that food security is not guaranteed](#)," February 25, 2021.

30 Federal Executive, "[Don't Expect to Charge Your Electric Vehicle at the Stations USPS Plans to Build](#)," April 23, 2023.

31 International Viewpoint, "[International food crisis and proposals to overcome it](#)," December 27, 2022.

32 IZA World of Labor, "[How to improve participation in social assistance programs](#)," December 2014.

33 E. Bardach and E. Eric M. Patashnik, *[A Practical Guide for Policy Analysis: The Eightfold Path to More Effective Problem Solving, 7th ed.](#)*, Appendix B: Things Governments Do, 2023.

34 USDA Economic Research Service, "[The Food and Nutrition Assistance Landscape: Fiscal Year 2021 Annual Report](#)," June 2022.

## Endnotes

35 White House, "Biden-Harris Administration National Strategy on Hunger, Nutrition, and Health," September 2022.

36 Center on Budget and Priorities, "WIC Works: Addressing the Nutrition and Health Needs of Low-Income Families for More Than Four Decades," January 2021.

37 Food Research & Action Center, "Making WIC Work Better: Strategies to Reach More Women and Children and Strengthen Benefits Use," May 2019.

38 Food Research & Action Center, "Bills We're Supporting," 2022. See more information about each at congress.gov.

39 Oregon.gov, "Food Insecurity Logic Model," January 2018.

40 Food Research & Action Center, "Making WIC Work Better: Strategies to Reach More Women and Children and Strengthen Benefits Use," May 2019.

41 The Marginalian, "How to Make Difficult Decisions: Benjamin Franklin's Pioneering Pros and Cons Framework,"

42 A. Vasan, C. C. Kenyon, C. Feudtner, A. G. Fiks, and A. S. Venkataramani. "Association of WIC Participation and Electronic Benefits Transfer Implementation," *JAMA Pediatr.* 175, no. 6(2021): 609–616. https://doi.org/10.1001/jamapediatrics.2020.6973.

43 Molly Sheridan and Coline Ferrant, "Participation in the Women, Infants and Children (WIC) Program: A Synthesis of the Literature,"2022, hal-03521082.

44 National Archives Office of the Federal Register, Executive Order 12291, Accessed December 2023.

45 Discounting in economics means that we lower the value of future costs or benefits because we think things in the future are less certain and less desirable than things in the present. So I'd rather have $100 today than $100 in the future because, for example, the cost of bread might be more than it is today.

46 A. Boardman et al., *Cost-Benefit Analysis: Concepts and Practice*, 5th ed., July 2018.

47 WIC, "About WIC: How WIC Helps," accessed December 2022.

48 S. Avruch and A. P. Cackley, "Savings achieved by giving WIC benefits to women prenatally," *Public Health Rep.* 110, no. 1 (Jan–Feb 1995): 27–34, PMID: 7838940; PMCID: PMC1382070.

49 WIC, "WIC data tables," accessed December 2022.

50 Paul A. Buescher, Linnea C. Larson, M. D. Nelson Jr, and Alice J. Lenihan, "Prenatal WIC participation can reduce low birth weight and newborn medical costs: a cost-benefit analysis of WIC participation in North Carolina," *Journal of the American Dietetic Association* 93, no. 2 (1993): 163–166.

51 Government Accountability Office, "Early Intervention: Federal Investments Like WIC Can Produce Savings," Apr 07, 1992, GAO-HRD-92-18.

52 C. Barnes and S. Petry, S., "'It Was Actually Pretty Easy': COVID-19 Compliance Cost Reductions in the WIC Program," *Public Admin Rev* 81 (2021): 1147–1156.

53 Statista, "Average quarterly cost per ride of ridesharing services in the United States from 2017 to 2019," accessed December 2022.

54 WIC, "WIC data tables," accessed December 2022.

55 National Public Radio, "A Looming Disaster: New Data Reveal Where Flood Damage Is An Existential Threat," February 22, 2021.

56 U.S. Department of Homeland Security, "Natural Disasters: Flooding," accessed December 2022.

57 Smithsonian, "Federal Flood Maps Are Outdated Because of Climate Change, FEMA Director Says," September 9, 2022.

58 American Flood Coalition, "Turning the tide toward equity: improving federal flood programs to serve marginalized populations," May 2020.

59 American Flood Coalition, "Elevating social equity in flooding and disaster recovery," August 2020.

60 FEMA, "NFIP's Pricing Approach," accessed December 2023.

61 Nagel, Stuart S. "Efficiency, Effectiveness, and Equity in Public Policy Evaluation." *Review of Policy Research* 6, no. 1 (August 1986): 99–120.

62 ClimateWire, "Hundreds of thousands drop flood insurance as rates rise," August 17, 2022.

63 White House, "Executive Order on Advancing Racial Equity and Support for Underserved Communities Throughout the Federal Government," EO 13985, January 20, 2021.

64 Annie E. Casey Foundation, "Embracing Equity: 7 Steps to Advance and Embed Race Equity and Inclusion Within Your Organization," 2014.

65 Ibid.

66 *The Guardian*, "Why are major beverage companies refusing to use a 90% recycled can?" October 30, 2014.

67 Brookings, "Politicians need to square with the American people on gasoline prices," April 20, 2022.

68 AAA, "Americans Are Driving Less Due to High Gas Prices," August 1, 2022.

69 Gallup, "Gas Prices Squeezing Americans as More Rate Economy 'Poor,'" June 28, 2022.

70 Gross, S. "Politicians need to square with the American people on gasoline prices," Commentary, Brookings, April 20, 2022.

# Endnotes

71 William Coplin and Michael O'Leary, *Everyman's Prince: A Guide to Understanding Your Political Problems*, 1972; "Teaching Political Strategy Skills with PRINCE," *Policy Analysis* 2, no. 1 (Winter 1976): 145–60.

72 *Mississippi Today*, "Welfare recipient won't stop fighting for 'decency and common sense'," December 21, 2022.

73 National Academies of Sciences, Engineering, and Medicine. 2007. *Rising Above the Gathering Storm: Energizing and Employing America for a Brighter Economic Future*. Washington, DC: National Academies Press. https://doi.org/10.17226/11463.

74 Ibid.

75 White House, "Remarks of President Barack Obama—As Prepared for Delivery, Address to Joint Session of Congress," Tuesday, February 24, 2009.

76 National Academies reports are available through the National Academies Press.

77 RAND policy analysis is available through their publications.

78 Congressional Research Service reports are available on almost any topic you might imagine. Only recently, however, have they become easily accessible to the public. Today you can find them on this website. You can find older reports, often quite useful, on other sites, particularly that of the Federation of American Scientists. One important item to note is that CRS reports are updated on a regular basis (unlike National Academies reports) so you should always check to make sure you have the most recent report if you find it on a site other than that of CRS.

79 Finding federal advisory committee reports can sometimes be challenging due to changing administrations. Here are the PCAST reports from the Obama Administration.

80 The FAO has a useful guide on policy briefs. I particularly like this FAO policy brief: "Achieving the Sustainable Development Goals requires investing in rural areas."

81 The Broad Research Communication Lab provides useful guidance for writing a policy memo.

82 Resources for the Future, "Explainers," accessed January 2023.

83 MOST Policy Initiative, "Legislative Science Notes," accessed January 2023.

84 Broad Research Communication Lab has a good overview of a policy elevator pitch that can help you prepare.

85 Here are two examples written by former students: Jennifer L. Brown et al., "Why Are Police Using a World War I–Era Chemical Weapon on Civilians?" *Scientific American*, April 20, 2021; Evvan Morton et al., "Removing Carbon From the Atmosphere Must Be Part of Climate Change Policy," *Issues in Science and Technology*, June 10, 2021.

86 [Merriam-Webster Dictionary](#).

87 Ibid.

88 [Merriam-Webster Dictionary](#).

89 American Geophysical Union, "[Words Matter](#)," October 17, 2011, based on "[Communicating the Science of Climate Change](#)," by Richard C. J. Somerville and Susan Joy Hassol, from *Physics Today*, October 2011, p. 48.

90 AGU, "[Watch your Words](#)," inspired by Hassol, S. J. (2008). "Improving how scientists communicate about climate change," *Eos, Transactions American Geophysical Union* 89(11), 106–107.

91 Scienceandpublic.com, [Dejargonzier](#) developed by Tzipora Rakedzon, Elad Segev, Noam Chapnik, Roy Yosef, and Ayelet Baram-Tsabari (2017). Automatic jargon identifier for scientists engaging with the public and science communication educators, *PLOS ONE*, August 9, 2017, http://journals.plos.org/plosone/article?id=10.1371/journal.pone.0181742.

92 University of Arizona, "[Writing Clearly & Concisely](#)," accessed January 2023.

93 University of Arizona, "[Writing Clearly & Concisely](#)," accessed January 2023.

94 [Merriam-Webster Dictionary](#).

95 Katie Langin, "[In a first, U.S. private sector employs nearly as many Ph.D.s as schools do](#)," *Science*, March 12, 2019.

96 Modified from Mark Bayer, ["How to effectively communicate your science to any audience"](#) and ["Infographic – 11 Keys for Translating Complex Topics."](#)

97 Chris Tyler, "[Top 20 things scientists need to know about policy-making](#)," *The Guardian*, December 2, 2013.

98 This table is largely based on suggestions from E. Suhay, E. Cloyd, E. Heath, and E. Nash, "[Recommended Practices for Science Communication with Policymakers](#)."

99 Melanie Zanona and Ella Nilsen, "[GOP push to shake label of climate crisis denier runs into Trump](#)," CNN, November 5, 2021.

100 Blake Ellis and Melanie Hicken, "[Republicans have unlikely allies in their fight to restrict abortion at the state level: Democrats](#)," CNN, September 6, 2022.

101 [Merriam Webster.](#)

102 [Scholar](#)

103 [Newton's Laws](#)

104 [Euclid's axioms](#)

# Endnotes

105 "[harmonizing sentiments of the day](#)"

106 [Science: The Endless Frontier](#)

107 Roger Pielke Jr., "[Five Modes of Science Engagement](#)," blog, January 19, 2015.

108 National Women's Hall of Fame, "[Frances Oldham Kelsey](#)," accessed 2022.

109 Markkula Center for Applied Ethics, "[Rachel Carson](#)," accessed 2022.

110 Carlie Porterfield, "[Dr. Fauci On GOP Criticism: 'Attacks On Me, Quite Frankly, Are Attacks On Science,'](#)" *Forbes*, December 10, 2021.

111 NASEM, "[NAS and NAM Presidents Alarmed By Political Interference in Science Amid Pandemic](#)," September 20, 2020.

112 Modified from a table in Science, "[Politics, science and public attitudes: What we're learning, and why it matters](#)," February 25, 2015, summarizing a collection of papers on "[The Politics of Science](#)" in *Annals of the American Academy of Political and Social Science*, March 2015.